THRIVING IN THE MIDST OF CHANGE

*Leading Authorities Share Their Best Secrets
for Discovering Opportunity, Prosperity and Peace
in Your Hyper-Changing Life —
Both Personally and Professionally*

Compiled by Doug Smart

James &
Brookfield
J&B
Publishers

THRIVING IN THE MIDST OF CHANGE

Managing Editor: Gayle Smart
Editor: Sara Kahan
Proofing Editor: Laura Johnson
Book Designer: Paula Chance
Copyright ©2002

For more information, contact:
James & Brookfield Publishers
P.O. Box 768024
Roswell, GA 30076
✆ 770-587-9784

Library of Congress Catalog Number 2001099872

ISBN: 0-9712851-2-8

10 9 8 7 6 5 4 3 2 1

CONTENTS

SHED OR YOU'RE DEAD: THRIVING IN THE MIDST OF CHANGE IS YOUR CHOICE

by Kathy Dempsey

They told me I was going to die. That Wednesday afternoon in May 1987 would never be forgotten. My ears burned as Dr. Gazaleh blurted out, "Kathy, your AIDS test . . . it's come back positive!"

As I hung up the phone, a tremor started through my hands, and then it accelerated through the rest of my body.

I was in shock. My worst nightmare had come true. I was a nurse working in the ER in June 1986 when an accident-related trauma patient was wheeled in. We had to crack open his chest to perform internal CPR. My hands had been wrist-deep inside him. But despite our best efforts, he died minutes later.

Later that night, we found out he had AIDS. My own heart skipped a beat as I looked down at my hands and remembered a minor cut on my right index finger. Believe it or not, back in the mid-80s we didn't wear latex gloves to protect us.

Because of the exposure, the doctors decided to test me every three months for a year. After three negative tests, I thought I was home free. I was wrong!

After the dreadful call, I rushed to the hospital to meet with the doctors. My head was spinning. I couldn't think. My hands were shaking so much I could barely grip the steering wheel.

This just couldn't be true. Why me? I was a nurse — trying to help a patient. I was not ready to die! I was just 26 years old.

The doctors decided to run additional tests to confirm the positive results. My nightmare continued. Two weeks later, the confirmatory tests also came back positive. The doctors notified the Centers for Disease Control (CDC), now also concerned. You see, I was the first healthcare worker in America to ever test HIV positive from an on-the-job exposure.

AIDS, just six years after it was discovered in May 1981, remained a guaranteed death sentence. Most AIDS victims did not survive more than a year. People feared AIDS as they used to fear leprosy, maybe more. Speculation was rampant, but no one really knew all the ways it could be spread.

No, this can't happen to me, I angrily thought. I can't handle it! What am I going to do? Not only am I HIV positive, but now it looks like I'm going to be a media spectacle — a poster child for the CDC. It was more than I could bear.

Reluctantly, that night, I sat down and told my family. A family of faith in a community that sometimes saw the disease as a curse, my Mom and Dad and sister, Virginia, were supportive.

Then, after mentally laboring for days, I forced myself to tell my boss. Dr. McGuire was sympathetic, but said, "Kathy, if this gets out, this hospital will shut down. I'm sorry, but you can't work here anymore."

I shared the shocking news with my church that weekend. To my amazement, some members turned away from me. They said AIDS is God's punishment for the gays! That I was not gay and that I had contracted HIV by trying to help someone seemed to escape their attention. Even some of my friends became distant. I guess they were afraid of catching the disease from me.

I stopped eating. I stopped sleeping. One night in a graduate school class, as I wrestled with my own demons, my professor announced a film, *Living with AIDS*. Sitting in the classroom, chest tight and head spinning, I watched young people at the prime of their lives waste away in hospitals. My classmates talked in horror of the disease. Little did they know who was sitting beside them.

That night I determined one thing: I was not going to die the slow, agonizing death of an AIDS victim. I was not going to waste away. I could not! I would not! I decided I would choose how I would die.

After class, I started driving, until I found myself in the parking lot of Chattanooga's most famous hotel. I was about to add to its legend!

My mind started racing. It raced for hours around a track called "regrets." Regrets of not spending more time with my family and friends. I was always too busy, too stressed. Regrets of not taking the time to find out who Kathy Dempsey was. All alone, I sat in my car that dark, drizzling night, with a bottle of sleeping pills in my hand. I was a nurse. I knew what it took . . . .

I was jolted back into reality by three knocks on my car window. It was Robin, one of my friends, from out of nowhere. "Kathy, are you OK?" she asked.

With tears streaming down my face, I despairingly shook my head, "No. I am scared and lonely." Robin climbed into the car beside me. We talked. We cried. It went on for hours.

But now, with Robin's intervention, caring, and support, I found I had the strength inside me that I needed to go forward. From her, and from others whose love and support I'd forgotten, I found my hope, as well!

But, the story doesn't end there.

Three months after my initial test, I received another phone call from Dr. Gazelah. "Kathy, I am not sure how to tell you this . . . but your tests, all eight of your tests, have come back negative. The CDC says you don't have AIDS!"

As I hung up the phone, I felt like a thousand-pound weight had been lifted from my chest.

Some people call it a medical error; I call it a miracle. What a gift! I had thought my life was over . . . and now I had it back. It was like a VCR and I got to push "reset." All those regrets, now I could do something about them. I thanked God and promised myself from that day forward, "I will not live my life the same way again."

So you might ask, "Kathy, what did you do differently after your AIDS scare?"

Well, I woke up. Insanely, I had been sleeping for 26 years. I had been given the wake-up call of my life. Now, it was my choice whether I was going to hit the snooze button or not. Not everyone gets a second chance; I thought I'd better take advantage of it.

That personal trauma, I found, was indeed a blessing, and God had a purpose for me from it. From that moment forward, I began to remake my life, to find ways to create a legacy: to leave the world a better place for Kathy's having been a part of it.

Let me benchmark my progress in what had become my own philosophy of life, and the personal journey I'd taken, by sharing my journal entry dated July 29, 1998.

"It was 7 a.m. Time for our quarterly ethics meeting at the hospital. As I rushed into the room at the last minute, I ran into a guy I hadn't seen in a while. 'Good Morning David, and how are you?'"

"I am fine, Kathy . . . but my lizard is dead."

Startled yet intrigued, I asked, "Your lizard is dead. What happened?"

"He didn't shed his skin . . . and if lizards don't shed their skin, they die."

"Why?" I asked curiously.

He explained patiently. "Lizards grow by shedding their skin. If they don't shed their skin, they aren't growing. Lizards die if they don't grow."

After I thought for a moment, I asked, "David what can we learn from the lizard?"

With a perplexed look on his face, he thought for a moment. "We all need to grow, we need to grow physically, mentally, spiritually . . . and how we grow is to shed our old skin. If we don't grow as humans, we'll die."

"And David, what does our old skin represent? Maybe old habits, negative thoughts, unhealthy relationships?"

Simultaneously, we looked at each other . . . the light bulb had gone on . . . "Shed or you're dead!"

Two things had happened that day. First, I had a benchmark for my own personal growth.

Second, because perhaps God had put David in my path that day, I had a metaphor — "Shed or You're Dead," featuring Lenny the Lizard, who soon would become my life's companion and my personal vehicle for helping others.

Shedding is growing, Lenny tells people, because on one side, it's letting go of the old; on the other side, it's gaining the new.

What causes us to shed?

Change!

Change is an inevitable phenomenon, a given, a fact of life. Yet most of us, in varying degrees fear change. Why? Because it's painful! But pain is part of life, and life is all about letting go of the loss in order to gain something new.

We live in a world that is rapidly accelerating, a world demanding a little more than the day before, a world where change seems to be our only constant.

Whether it's a death, birth, divorce, marriage, loss of job, new job, broken relationship, new love, financial hardship, financial gain, getting sick, or getting well, it's all about change . . . it's all about shedding.

As humans, we've been given the wonderful gift of choice. And shedding is all about choice. Sometimes, like me, you need a jolt to help motivate you into making healthier choices. My wake-up call taught me three important lessons.

Be Yourself

Who was I? I didn't know. Most of my life, I had tried to be what I thought everyone else wanted me to be — trying to please others, trying to be accepted. As I was growing up, I always wanted to be someone else. Some days it was Cindy, the homecoming queen. Some days it was Brenda, the valedictorian. Some days it was Pam, the MVP. For some reason, I never wanted to be simply Kathy.

It had taken a crisis in my life to shake me up and help me realize that I needed to be "myself." One problem: I did not know who I was. I had never spent the time exploring myself. I had always been too busy "doing." Regretfully, I had never taken the opportunity to get to know the one person who was going to be with me for the rest of my life: ME! I made a commitment to spend some time finding out who I was.

Here are a few things that worked for me: My first step was to seek counseling. Scared to death, I knew I had to do it. I had to learn to be. Zig Ziglar once told me you must "be" before you can "do" and "do" before you can "have."

The next step was identifying my purpose, my passion, and my mission in life. Then I developed goals. Finally, I decided to set my own guidelines for living and to filter everything I do through the light of my personal mission:

- To love myself and to love others
- To grow myself and to help others grow
- To enjoy life and glorify God

The last few years have taught me that I function best when I follow my guidelines. I get into trouble when I don't.

Everyone is a unique and creative individual. Be yourself.

Enourage Others

I am alive today because a few people encouraged me. Many people during my crisis rejected and alienated themselves from me. We don't have to live very long before life hands us more than a few crises. Encouragement and support lightens the burden, not only in crisis, but also in our everyday lives. Here are a few suggestions:

- Expect the best out of people. People have a tendency to live up to what we think of them.
- Offer the gift of presence — not saying or doing, but just being there for someone. Listen.
- Ask people what they need. So often in life we make assumptions about what others need. Ask them. You will be surprised. They will tell you.

- Make people feel important. People have a great need to feel valued, respected and significant. Address people with their names. Imagine everyone you meet is wearing a sign that reads: "MAKE ME FEEL IMPORTANT." Praise people ten times more than you criticize them.

- Support the person, process the mistakes and celebrate the victories. A mistake is not a failure if you learn something from it. When someone makes a mistake, support and help him or her to learn from it and decide what to do differently next time. Then, when success comes, celebrate! Revel in other people's accomplishments.

I had the privilege of working at Memorial Hospital in Chattanooga for seven years. When I think of encouragement, I think of someone very special at Memorial. Her name is Jessica Branch. Jessica is a wonderful person. She is everything you would ever imagine in a friend. She is kind, generous, thoughtful, considerate, and helpful. Everyone at Memorial loves her. A few years ago, the house of an employee burned down. Everything was destroyed. Jessie rallied everyone together and gave the employee money and clothes to start over.

Then, a few months later, I was having a rough week. I arrived at work and walked into my office. There on my desk was a vase of flowers. The attached note said, "Just thinking about you. Have a great day. Jessica Branch." In seconds, my spirit was lifted from discouragement to encouragement. This little gift of thoughtfulness made my day!

The truth is Jessica Branch is not "someone" at Memorial Hospital; she is "everyone." She is an encouraging spirit that pervades the culture. And although Jessica is not real-life flesh and blood, she is alive and well. Her spirit is what makes Memorial Hospital the special place that it is.

When people come to work at Memorial, they are asked to be a Jessica. They are asked to look for opportunities to encourage others.

An interesting phenomenon occurs when you encourage others: The more you encourage others, the more you are encouraged. It has often been said, "Give people what they need, and they will give you what you need." Encouragement: We can't get enough of it.

Enjoy Life

My greatest lesson was to enjoy life. I had never fully appreciated life until I looked death straight in the face. I had always taken health for granted and assumed I would live a long, prosperous life. I had assumed I had all the time in the world. Since my health crisis, I have learned to enjoy life by:

- Being in the moment. Not replaying the past or worrying about the future, but living in the moment. Ninety percent of what we worry about never happens.

- Living life to the fullest. Balancing work and play. Some of the happiest people in life are the ones who successfully blend the two. I began by making a list of places I wanted to go in my lifetime — things I wanted to do — things I wanted to accomplish.

- Facing fears. Most people's greatest barriers are themselves. Fearing failure, I had never taken many risks. I found that truly facing my fear and moving through it not only injected me with confidence but also provided me with new opportunities. When fear floods my mind, I try to ask myself, "What is the worst thing that could happen?" Some of my greatest fears have now become my greatest pleasures.

- Spending energy carefully. We have only a finite amount of energy to spend each day. Too often I allowed other people to spend mine. But why? I wouldn't allow other people to spend my money. I identified my personal sources of fuel and arranged them into my daily schedule. Now I have a mechanism to continually replenish my energy supplies.

- Living passionately. Life is unpredictable. None of us knows for sure if we are going to be here tomorrow. All we have is today. Are you doing what you love to do? What are you passionate about? So often, I have heard people say, "Just ten more years and I can retire and do what I really love to do."

Why wait? I had wasted many years of my life doing things I didn't enjoy. I have since discovered the real joy in life comes in living your passion.

There are many things we do not have control over, but we do have a choice to be ourselves, to encourage others, and to enjoy life. Because of my traumatic experience, I know what is important in life. I know where to focus. I know, more than ever, that shedding is a choice.

What happens if you choose not to shed?

"The tragedy of man is what dies inside of himself while he still lives."
—Albert Schweitzer

It was like clockwork. Friday night at 10 p.m., the Emergency Room doors flew open and in rolled Medic 5. The squeaky wheels of the stretcher stopped abruptly at my triage desk.

"Where should I put him?" Paramedic Stone announced as he handed me the ambulance report.

"Just place him on the stretcher in the hallway," I automatically responded.

It was George . . . again. It was the same song and dance every Friday night. George was a disheveled 46-year-old man. For the past four years, he had qualified for the ER frequent flyer program. Every week he would come in intoxicated, then he'd lie in the hallway until he sobered up enough for the police to take him to jail.

"Here we go again," I thought to myself as I held my breath to care for him. With his foul mouth, matted hair stuck to the sheets, unshaven beard, and urine stained pants, he was one of the most challenging patients I'd ever had to handle. Week after week my irritation with George swelled as I continued to help a man, who for some reason, wasn't helping himself.

One Friday night, the ER doors flew open as they typically did, but this time something was different. It was George — but this time he walked in. I was in shock! Slowly George approached my triage desk and sat down.

Feeling a bit awkward, I began taking his vital signs. Although I knew George well, I had never had a face-to-face conversation with him when he was sober. As I took the blood pressure cuff off his arm, I thought to myself, I have to know. I must find out.

Finally, I mustered the courage and asked, "George, you have been coming in here drunk every week for years. It's the same story every time; you lie on the stretcher till you sober up enough to be hauled off to jail. Please, help me understand why."

He paused for a second and took a deep breath; then with his voice trembling, he slowly looked up at me as his eyes began to water.

"Kathy," he said, "I know you might find this hard to believe, but once I was a very successful businessman in this town. Several years ago my wife and two children were driving home, and another car went out of control and hit them head on. They all died instantly. I couldn't handle the pain. I couldn't deal with it. I started drinking to cope."

"The drinking got so bad that I eventually lost my job, then my house, then I ended up on the streets."

As tears streamed down his face, he said, "I died too!"

My heart sank. What a tragedy.

George was right. Although he was not in the car the night of the accident, he did die, too. Not physically (although his drinking was damaging his body) but emotionally, mentally, socially, financially, and spiritually, George was dead.

Through this tragic event, he had become stuck. He had been unable to shed. My heart went out to him because, for some reason, he had made a choice not to get help.

Most of us won't experience the tragic loss of our entire family as George did, but who is to say how our lives will unfold. We can't predict life events, but we can control our responses to them. We can decide that, no matter what life hands us, we will make the choice to thrive in the midst of change. And if we get stuck, we will get help. Below are some tips to help deal with change.

Lenny's Skin Shedding Tips to
Thriving in the Midst of Change

1. Recognize you have 100% control over your response.
2. Identify what you are grateful for.
3. Be honest with yourself and others.
4. Get the facts.
5. Develop a plan.
6. Ask yourself: What is the worst thing that could happen?
7. Ask yourself: What is the best thing that could happen?
8. Utilize appropriate outlets for your feelings (i.e., anger).
9. Identify your resources — family and friends, money, skills. If needed, get help.
10. Commit to becoming a "learning individual."
11. Identify and prioritize the issues.
12. Laugh!
13. Search (maybe even dig) for the lesson.
14. Avoid negative people.
15. Help someone else — encourage others.
16. Take care of yourself — eat properly, sleep, exercise.
17. Let GO!
18. Get excited about the possibilities.
19. Be yourself (discover your passion and values).
20. Anticipate change and accept it as a natural part of growth.

"In times of change, those who shed will inherit the earth.
Those who refuse to shed will find themselves
well-equipped for a life that no longer exists."

— Lenny the Lizard

Remember, it's your CHOICE!

ABOUT
KATHY DEMPSEY

*C*ontact *Kathy if you are interested in helping your organization grow through change and change through growth. Kathy's truly unique experiences make her one of America's most sought after speakers, writers and facilitators on issues of change, organizational development and strategic planning. Best known for her creative, unique, and innovative approach, her presentations are engaging, highly interactive and full of fun — many of them incorporating her popular "Shed or You're Dead" approach. Kathy was responsible for leading Memorial Health Care System's (named a Top 100 Hospital in the United States) organizational development efforts. She is President of The Learning Agenda, a company that helps individuals and organizations grow by "shedding their skin." Kathy is also co-author of* Irresistible Leadership. *The Georgia Speakers Association voted her the 1999 Showcase Speaker of the Year. Bob Pike's Creative Training Techniques International also named her the 1999 Trainer of the Year. Some of her clients include American Express, Delta Air Lines, Habitat for Humanity, Lucent Technologies, The American Red Cross, South Carolina Bankers Association, DeKalb Medical Center, AFC Enterprises (Cinnabons, Popeye's Chicken, Seattle's Best Coffee) and the Georgia Society of Association Executives.*

Contact information:
Kathy Dempsey
The Learning Agenda
8317 Hamilton Oaks Drive
Chattanooga, TN 37421
Phone: (423) 894-8585
Fax: (423) 894-0071
E-mail: Kathy@TheLearningAgenda.com
Website: www.TheLearningAgenda.com

Six Steps You Can Take to Navigate Change and Create Your Own Desired Future

by Sam Waltz

"**S**am, how is it you've maintained the resilience to accomplish what you have in light of the issues you've faced in your life?" the Governor asked me a few weeks ago. We were relaxing in a skybox on a marvelous summer evening, enjoying the Wilmington Blue Rocks, our local minor league baseball team.

I looked into the face of this 70-plus-year-old man whom I've known, respected, and cared for since 1986. That's when the DuPont Company had assigned me to be public affairs issues manager, policy assistant, and speech writer to him when he was senior vice president and head of one of DuPont's most important $2 billion strategic business units.

In the intervening years, we've become mutual friends, confidantes, and counselors. Our lives have taken us in interesting directions since, with challenges for each of us too complex and perhaps too irrelevant to recount here, and our paths crossed many, many times.

After he ended his DuPont career to become a cabinet secretary, he subsequently served as lieutenant governor and governor of our state. Today, he represents a prominent east coast law firm in its business relationship issues in China, invests in enterprises and people in which he believes, serves on numerous boards, and adds value to the lives of family and friends.

After I left DuPont in 1993, I founded, and still run, two business-es and, in 1999 at the age of 51, became the nationally elected head of our industry and its professional society. I write often, speak around the country and the world, counsel others, invest, and serve on a few boards of my own.

Work — Life Counsel is a Legacy Builder

"Governor," I said, "I have no secrets. What I have learned, I have learned from you and from hundreds of other extraordinary people with whom God has blessed me.

"In fact, His real blessing to me, Governor, is that today my work is about what I love, which is creating a legacy, to share some of those eternal truths with others, with friends and with clients who have become friends, just as you and I have!

"Who could ask for more blessings than that?"

The Governor smiled and nodded, and we turned back for a moment to watch our home team create the visitor's third out, so we each could stand for the seventh inning stretch, enroute to the night's victory.

As the shadows crept across the outfield that evening, it occurred to me that few of us take enough time in our lives to stretch, and to reflect. The Governor's question gave me the impetus to record some ideas — some of the cumulative wisdom at this tender point in my life — that I share with friends and clients.

Some people feel the world is divided between men and women. Or between old and young. Or between Yankees and Southerners. Or city dwellers and suburbanites and rural folk. Or executives and workers. These are demographics, tangible things, about each of us as individuals that tell the world who we are.

But that's not really who we are. Who we are, in my view, is shaped by how we see the world, by our value systems, and by how we act.

The world is divided, in my view, between those people who feel they have surrendered their lives to destiny and those people who feel they can influence the important things in their lives. For the latter, "internal locus of control" is the term psychologists use to describe those who have the psychographics, what German sociologist Max Weber called the *Weltanschuung*, the world view, to influence the important issues in one's own life.

For some, if they get sick with an illness or disease, "it's God's will, and, if I get better, it was meant to be." However, Norman Cousins, years ago in his classic book, *Anatomy of an Illness*, recognized the influence of the individual will to shape her or his survival.

For others, if they are to become wealthy, it will occur because lightning strikes, and they win the lottery. The notion escapes them that each of us can create a financially successful future for self and family through our own enterprise.

Areas of relationships are a bit more "fuzzy," as a legion of writers from Naomi Wolf to Dr. Laura Schlesinger to Daniel Goleman suggest, and shaping our bodies and ourselves can be an unending source of frustration, as one of my favorite comic strip artists, Cathy Guisewaite, reminds us in "Cathy."

Visualizing: Creating a Plan from a Dream

Our friend Stephen Covey had it right, in *The 7 Habits of Highly Effective People*, with the first habit, "begin with the end in mind."

I'm not talking about some vague hope or dream of largesse and wellness. I'm talking about creating your own personal visualization — as a work plan with goals and strategies — that seems as rich in detail as a digital photo transmitted to your computer, one that you can enlarge and examine in each of the important areas.

Blow up those areas of dreams for your inspection. Try them on! What do they look like? How do they feel? Smell? Taste?

"The greatest tragedy in life is people who have sight but no vision," remarked Helen Keller, the blind woman who became one of our greatest inspirations.

Our lessons sometimes come from funny places in our lives. The power of visualization was not something that I learned in the hundreds of hours and thousands of dollars of training that DuPont invested in me. Rather, I learned it on the suburban softball field, with teen-aged girls, coaching my daughter Rachel's team over the years.

As each girl went to bat in a critical moment, I challenged her to visualize the ball being batted back through the infield, using all that we had worked on in practice. And, on defense, I coached the girls to visualize two things, "What do I do if the ball is hit to me, and what do I do if it's hit to someone else?"

In a recreational league where a lottery and draft effectively stocked each team equitably at the beginning of the season, spring after spring our team competed for the championship, essentially because these teen-aged girls learned to visualize during the game, and throughout the season, and execute our plan!

Reflection and Questioning is a Planning Cornerstone

How do we build that vision? In the problem-solving strategic planning we do for our clients, for themselves and their businesses, we make it a point — no, an act of principle — to point out that research and reflection precede planning and design. That means asking questions, lots of them.

Some colleagues in the planning and problem-solving industry like to suggest that strategic planning is a great mystical temple, where access is limited to only a sacred and learned priesthood elite.

Not so! Strategic planning — although it is a competency skill set of its own — is not rocket science. Whether in our business or personal lives, such planning consists of asking and answering three simple questions:

1. Where am I?
2. Where do I want to be?
3. How do I get there?

The reflection and self-assessment that accompany asking and answering these questions, and the planning that follows, can alter the course of our lives, which is what this chapter is about. On my bulletin board, next to my desk, I have posted for years quotes from three great thinkers about the value of questioning and reflection.

It was Aristotle who wrote, "It was through the feeling of wonder that people first began to question."

Socrates, the progenitor of the great Socratic method, wrote, "Since the soul has learned all things, there is nothing to prevent someone from discovering all the rest, if they are brave and do not grow tired of inquiring."

Plato, who occupied a similar niche with Socrates among the great thinkers, wrote, "We will be better and braver if we engage and inquire than if we indulge in the idle fancy that we already know."

Our Destiny is in Six Areas of Our Lives

The commitment that each of us should feel to lifelong learning needs to include an honesty in looking inwardly, to study self and situation!

I suggest to CEOs, executives, friends, and family that each of us look at six criteria in our own personal lives:

1. Spiritual: Ethical, Behavioral, and Moral
2. Physical: Wellness, Fitness, and Nutrition
3. Financial: Income, Worth, and Asset Creation
4. Relational: Family, Primary, and Extended
5. Professional: Work, Business, and Career
6. Personal: Growth and Self

It's been said that "a vision without action is called a daydream; but then again, action without a vision is called a nightmare." Stephen Covey's second principle is to have a predisposition to action, but, of course, starting with the end in mind. That's what we'll talk briefly about in each of the six areas of our lives.

Ultimately, as basketball great Michael Jordan once said, "Heart is what separates the good from the great." What we're talking about here is putting greatness — personal greatness — into each of our lives, and that takes heart!

Spiritual: Ethical, Behavioral, and Moral

For those of us who are Baby Boomers, we've seen the spiritual suffer the indignity of becoming passé. And we've seen its resurgence!

You don't race down the steps of a collapsing World Trade Center building without rediscovering some spiritual faith, or sit in the cockpit of a fighter jet over a Middle East terrorist enemy without a prayer that God's hand rests on your shoulder, and the shoulders of your colleagues and family. While the moments may not seem nearly as dramatic, each of us in our daily lives races down some important steps or sits in a dangerous cockpit!

How do you set a spiritual goal? Personally! For some, it may be church attendance. For others, it may be prayer. For others, it may be getting to heaven. For some, it may be adherence to the Ten Commandments. For yet others, it may be shared faith among family and friends. For some, it is good works.

For me, I was raised a Christian in a small East Central Illinois farm town, where my faith was important to me. At 22, in 1969, when I married a girl not of a similar faith while away from home during Vietnam-era US Army Intelligence Command service, the accommodations we later made to build a successful marriage over most of our 27 years together led me to permit the diminishment of my faith and my religion in my life. It was my own choice, and no one else's, but I was wrong to let the spiritual side of my life dissipate.

Today, while I do enjoy a broad and inclusive view of faith and spirituality, my striving in my goal-setting is to reestablish and nourish a personal connection with God. You can, too, whatever your faith. Your goals should be your own goals, and no one else's! Although, ideally, you'll want them to embrace your family, and your family will embrace them with you.

Physical: Wellness, Fitness, and Nutrition

For most of us, it's a bit easier to be specific with regard to physical and body wellness than with spirituality. Health embodies a number of components, including freedom from disease, fitness, exercise, weight, and nutrition.

Admittedly, a few things occur that we cannot control, including some cancers and genetic issues. Most of the contributing factors to disease, though, are personal, not environmental or genetic. The number of people who indulge complaints about speculative environmental issues (beyond their direct control!), while continuing to smoke or eat to the point of obesity or not follow a pattern of even moderate exercise, is astounding!

Criteria in which to set goals include:

1. *Create healthy habits*, including becoming tobacco-free. Studies show that the women and men who run the tobacco industry shorten the life of one in three addicts they create, and they reduce the quality of life for the balance. It's the greatest single plague that anyone has inflicted on us as Americans. That Americans are doing it to Americans — creating addicts to create billions in profits — is morally bankrupt, I feel. Obviously, being drug-free and using alcohol only in moderation, if at all, are givens. Buckle your seat belt. Don't drink and drive. Practice safe sex.

2. *Maintain a healthy weight.* Clinical obesity (20% or greater than your target weight) kills, and even lesser amounts of excess weight injure and shorten life, and reduce its quality, too.

3. *Exercise for fitness.* Daily. Moderation is okay. Just do something!

4. *Nutrition.* Eat well! Healthily! My own meat-and-potatoes Midwestern diet has its limits, particularly since I don't eat fish, but I've learned to be more careful about how I eat.

5. *Use and respect medical counsel.* See your physician regularly, at least annually after age 50, for physicals and checkups. And see that those you love are protected, too, starting with the March of Dimes regimen for good pre-natal care.

It doesn't require a PhD to know what you need to do. Recognize that each of these categories represents a choice you make each day, every day.

Financial: Income, Worth, and Asset Creation

In marriage, and in life, financial issues often are the greatest source of headaches and heartaches! And, yet, they're something about which each of us can do something. Unfortunately, society allows us — sometimes even encourages and rewards — a 'poor me' victim attitude about the lack of material means, and it is a passivity into which each person can be tempted.

My parents were sharecroppers on our Illinois farm, where we lived with an outhouse from 1947, when I was born, until 1958 when we moved to town. While we may have been poor, my brother, Dick, and I didn't feel poor, and we constantly and lovingly were urged to excel and achieve. Today, while neither my brother nor I would be regarded as wealthy by most standards, we're in control of our lives and managing our affairs well.

I encourage people to set and pursue objectives in three major categories:

1. *Income*, what you earn annually, salary for most people.
2. *Asset Creation*, the things you buy that hold value and, ideally, create income, e.g., stocks and bonds, real estate.
3. *Net Worth*, that is, the 'worth' of your family unit in assets.

One lesson I learned on the farm is that "you don't eat your seed corn." You can consume a kernel of corn today, and have nothing left tomorrow; or you can plant (save and invest) that seed kernel of corn today and generate two, three, or more ears of corn at the end of the season.

In his various books on building wealth, Robert Allen tells an incredible story about the power of compounding: $100 invested monthly between ages 20 and 35 can make you a millionaire at retirement, and the same $100 invested monthly between 50 and 65 doesn't make a dent in your needs.

Ultimately, your personal strategy is to move your reliance from salary-driven income to asset-driven income, where you have real freedom in your life, whether you do it by building a business, conserving your income, earning a generous pension, inheriting (or marrying!) money, taking great risks, or few risks.

Relational: Family, Primary, and Extended

The essential truth that each of us knows is the power of the relationships within our family unit, and with our friends, neighbors, and our various communities.

Our firm is located in a suburban office park, where, when we moved in, the former tenant's sign was large enough to allow more than our logo. So we were challenged to describe a bit more of what we do on our sign. Along with Research and Strategic Planning, we added Change Management, Reputation Management, and Relationship Management. That sign was put up in 1995, but even today, our firm is probably the only one in the Delaware Valley of Greater Philadelphia that lists Relationship Management as part of its offering.

Yet, as our work is more and more about what we call "creating desired behaviors," we have come to realize, and to coach our clients accordingly, that success in life and business is about creating win-win-win alignments with important stakeholders in order to achieved desired outcomes for all. Whether at home, or in business, happiness comes from creating win-win relationships with important stakeholders.

At home, it's done for love, in our roles as spouse and parent, child and sibling, friend and neighbor. At work, it's done for success in the business enterprise because it's the only way to create long-term healthy prosperity.

"Syntonics Relationship Management©" is what we call our branded Stakeholder Relationship Management process. Syntonics derives from an ancient Greek term that once meant "the active process of musical harmonization," e.g., two people actively harmonizing in song. In its etymological evolution, it came to mean "the active process of linguistic harmonization," e.g., two people actively communicating via creation of shared meanings.

We use Syntonics to mean creating win-win stakeholder relationship alignments, e.g., working to actively align and harmonize interests with important stakeholders (or family and friends). In the business world, we thoughtfully apply a 10-step process that essentially boils down to research, design, implementation, and evaluation.

Critical for each of us — at home, in our community and at work with colleagues and customers — is to map the relationships that are important. Then we need to understand where we are, where each relationship is weak or strong. Alongside that, we need to understand the needs, wants and values of the other person(s), and the implications for us in creating more effective win-win alignments that help each of us succeed, whether the motivation is love or money or altruism.

Professional: Work, Business, and Career

My children are Sam III, 24, Rachel, 22, and Andrew, 19. The time I've had to talk with them about work has been a joyful opportunity to reflect on what I've learned since I drew my first paycheck in June 1965 as a student sports PR assistant at the University of Illinois.

During my 16-year career as a corporate PR exec at DuPont, I knew a lot of people who set their goals to become a manager, director, or vice president by certain points in their lives and careers. I also saw that single-minded goal-setting created a lot of unhappy people, some who achieved their goals and many who did not.

In addition to our client work, I meet at least once or twice weekly with friends, and friends of friends, who are — as I describe them — "in transition." Some lessons I've learned that I share include:

1. *Lifelong Learning* — it's your only way to be successful throughout your life.

2. *Flexibility* — the chances are that you will set out to do one

thing at 20, and at 30, 40, 50 and 60 you'll be doing entirely different things — different each decade!

3. *Happiness* — understand what in your work life and work day makes you happy. Is it about money? Workplace relationships? A sense of mission to society? Intensity? I sometimes find myself quoting that popular writer and speaker, Harvey Mackay, who said, "Find something you love to do and you'll never have to work a day in your life." It's important to understand the difference between success — when you get what you want — and happiness, when you want what you have.

Balance of Properties is a term we used at DuPont to describe products. With certain properties, you get certain features and benefits. One feature may help a product last longer, but it increases the price, or perhaps it makes it less comfortable to the touch. Others may "feel good," but not have the resilience for durability.

Work, jobs, careers, and life can be a lot like that, when certain things that may seem desirable (e.g., high salary) may come with other things that a particular person finds undesirable (e.g., rigid hierarchies, reduced personal satisfaction, politics, ethical issues).

Personal: Growth and Self

Finally, last but not least, is a focus on self. Those around you — at home, at work, and in your community — won't be happy with you if you're not happy with you. Ultimately, it's each of us who is responsible for her/his own happiness, not those around us!

It's important to understand and adopt the mental attitudes that help you succeed, and to discard the ones that drag you down. One wise person said "We're just about as happy as we make up our minds to be," and I'm convinced he was right.

I've seen people of wealth suffer as individuals, and I heard recently of one retired wealthy corporate senior executive who ended up clinically depressed and institutionalized because of the decline in his paper wealth with the stock market's implosion of 2000-01. And yet each of us knows of people who live happily in poverty, or next to it.

Attitude, in fact, touches each one around us, at work and at home. "People want to know how much you care before they care how much you know," wrote James F. Hind. In my experience, all other things being equal (ethics, competency, etc.), nothing compensates for enthusiasm, energy, and a positive mental attitude. Cynicism is the greatest corrupting force that we face as individuals and organizations, I feel, because cynicism lowers our expectations of those around us, and, ultimately it lowers our expectations of ourselves.

Having said that, how do we design a positive attitude about self into our lives? A few thoughts for your use in life planning:

1. *Understand the importance of personal integrity and ethical behavior.* Happiness comes from creating win-win-win outcomes around you. If your success now comes from winning at someone else's expense, a win-lose, you're headed down a path of unhappiness, heartache, and discontent.

2. *Understand what makes you happy and contented* — via a frank discussion with the real you (in reflection) and with those you love — and build a positive, constructive plan towards that.

3. *Understand the sources of your emotional and psychological health*, and work on the areas that need work. Is one of them creating more emotional balance in your life?

4. *Focus positively on your personal growth as an individual,* within the context of lifelong learning. What areas most interest you, and how/where can you pursue them?

5. *Carve out time for you and for your interests!* So many of us spend so much time giving at work, and at home, and in our community, that we lose sight of who we are, and what we need to sustain and nourish ourselves. That includes time for reflection, recreation, rest, and renewal.

Build some self-awareness. Remember how Abraham Maslow

built his *Hierarchy of Needs,* with food and shelter at the bottom, rising on up through self-esteem and ultimately self-actualization, and understand where you are in the process. Perhaps, too, understanding your behavioral profiles via Myers-Briggs, or your DISC (Dominance, Influence, Supportiveness, Conscientiousness) from Inscape Publishing (formerly Carlson Learning) will help.

Creating Action by Creating Accountability

The best accountability ultimately is accountability to self, although often you create accountability in open discussions with those at home and work who are interested in your welfare. My favorite thought on that point, attributed in various forms to Henry Ford I, is, "Whether we think we can, or whether we think we cannot, we're right!"

Life is about navigating change, and about taking control of our lives. The status quo is our enemy, and inertia is its primary weapon. Personal triumph comes from vision, supported by commitment and goals, and executed with inertia-busting actions. That means declaring yourself, and your goals, to friends and family.

Yes, that does involve risk for each of us. Psychological risk, most often, because the pain of the unknown — for too many people — exceeds the pain of the known.

Half the worry in the world seems to be felt by people trying to make decisions before they feel they have sufficient knowledge. However, when it comes time to make an important decision, rarely do any of us have all the information we need to remove risk from the equation. We just have to learn to live with uncertainty! And we need to trust ourselves and our wits!

It's Time to Create Your Own Desired Future

Although I've lost track of the source of this comment, it is one of my favorites, and I quote it often:

"To laugh is to risk appearing the fool. To weep is to risk appearing sentimental. To reach out for another is to risk involvement. To expose feelings is to risk exposing your true self. To place your ideas, your dreams, before a crowd is to risk their loss. To love is to risk not being loved in return. To live is to risk dying. To hope is to risk failure.

"But risks must be taken. Because the greatest hazard in life is to risk nothing. If you risk nothing and do nothing, you dull your spirit. You may avoid suffering and sorrow, but you cannot learn, feel, change, grow, love, and live. Chained by your attitude, you are a slave. You have forfeited your freedom."

Let me close with this image, which comes from a favorite Norman Rockwell-type poster, of which I've seen several versions.

It features a scrawny 10-year-old boy, tossing a ball in his right hand, with a bat slung over his left shoulder, his ball glove hanging from the bat, walking along past a stockade-type fence, his shadow on the fence silhouetting his dreams. The shadow? It's of a well-muscled major league baseball player, finishing his home run swing as he propels the pitch over the outfield wall!

Each of us has such dreams in our lives. Our dreams are within our grasp if we're willing to make them our goals, to share them with those we love and care about, and to plan how to achieve them. Please let me know how you do with your dreams after reading this chapter. I do care!

ABOUT
SAM WALTZ

Some people know Sam Waltz as a business problem-solving strategist. Others know him as an executive coach and counselor. Others know him as a popular motivational speaker and writer. And just about all of them call him friend, cheerleader and confidante. Known as a coach and counselor to governors, senators, corporate CEOs, entrepreneurs, and our next generation's rising stars! A native of East Central Illinois farm country, he has lived in Delaware since 1975. Sam is a former political reporter, senior DuPont executive, and CEO and Chairman of the Public Relations Society of America (PRSA). A Vietnam-era veteran who worked in US Army Intelligence, Sam Waltz holds BS and MS degrees from the University of Illinois. His doctoral coursework in public policy was done at the University of Delaware. Sam's clients include Fortune 500 firms, the U.S. Air Force, Capitol Hill trade associations, universities, and leading not-for-profits.

Contact information:
Sam Waltz
Atlantic Leadership Institute
P.O. Drawer 3778
3920 Kennett Pike, Greenville Station
Wilmington, DE 19807-0778
Phone: (302) 777-4774
Fax: (302) 777-4775
E-mail: SamWaltz@SamWaltz.com
Website: www.AtlanticLeadership.com
www.SamWaltz.com

CHOOSE TO LIVE WITH GRACE

by Nancy Hedrick, M.B.A.

Gracie is my goldfish. Even if she is just your typical 25-cent garden variety goldfish, she is quite beautiful, her golden orange scales shimmering against the aqua blue marbles and lush, green plastic flora in her glass bowl. I found Gracie at a local pet store where she was swimming around in a large tank with a hundred of her goldfish friends. For some reason she called out to me over all the other fish, so I took her home with me. She had no choice in the matter. I decided to call her Gracie the Goldfish because I liked the alliteration, and *grace* has been a meaningful and memorable word all my life — more on that later. Since Gracie is a girl's name, I decided she was a she. She had no choice in that matter either.

At the time of the purchase, I had no idea of the important role Gracie was to play in my life. She has since become an inspiration to me! She is a constant reminder that, unlike Gracie, we humans have a "choice in the matter." Because we uniquely possess the gift of choice, we have choices in all matters and in all changes. At a minimum, we always have the ability to choose our attitude and response. Unfortunately, we too often misunderstand or misapply this gift, or simply forget we have it.

"You were given a lot of wonderful powers. You have the power to think, to love, to create, to imagine, to plan. The greatest power you have is the power to choose. Wherever you are today, you are there because you chose to be there."

— Lou Holtz

Why do we misunderstand, misapply or at times even forget our wonderful gift of choice? Most of us are too distracted and caught up in our daily lives — both personal and professional. Multiplying opportunities bring multiplying demands, which in turn bring increased stress. The danger is that when our lives are spinning in these circles, we become so stretched and weary that instead of *living by choice*, we begin to *live by chance*. And the more we relinquish our power of choice, the deeper we dig ourselves into the holes of exhaustion, lost confidence or indifference. Eventually our ability and even desire to use our gift of choice become rusty, making it even more difficult to deal with change.

"The tragedy of life is what dies inside a man while he lives."
— Albert Schweitzer

In my own corporate background throughout 1980s and 90s, I experienced times when the simmering employee attitude was one of just sliding by — working by chance. The insidiousness of that attitude reminds me of the "Creeping Jenny" weed that, as a child, I used to help my mom pull out by the root before it took over and choked her beautiful irises, tulips, and peonies.

Those times and pockets of dwindling motivation were due to many intertwining issues many of us have experienced. Cutbacks and layoffs are frequent in our increasingly competitive marketplaces. The uncertainty and change they bring diminish our sense of loyalty. Many of us who were lucky enough to survive the layoffs were left with twice the workload at the same paycheck. That, too, makes it difficult to embrace, much less, absorb change. Also, there were times when the lack of motivation to support and adapt to change stemmed from the lack of a clear vision to rally behind. Perhaps there was a vision and a mission, but in the haste of implementing and adjusting to the change, it was never fully shared or explained to all those affected.

In looking back over the last twenty-five years, it is amazing to realize that the incredible advances in technology designed to help us be more productive actually interfere at times with our ability to handle change. This brings to mind a paper I wrote in 1980 while in graduate school. The paper hypothesized a double-digit growth in the leisure industry based on the theory that technological advances would create time savings, which would result in more leisure time, and therefore more dollars spent on the leisure industry. The irony is that, rather than basking in the sun, we have used the time savings to take on more work. In the 1970's there was talk of an impending four-day work week. Now we operate in a "24/7" world with studies showing that we Americans work more hours per week since then, and more than any other industrialized nation. This is not necessarily bad in itself. However, at the same time, we have lost our occasional "slow times" or "downtimes" that helped us recuperate from major changes or periods with extra heavy workloads.

In 1981 when I began my career, there were natural downtimes where we could recover, guilt-free, from high-intensity periods — whether at the end of a project, the end of a quarter, or the end of the year. Data analysis and reporting were monthly or quarterly. But now all of this is virtually continuous. There is no longer any "catch-up" time, "slow season" and, sadly, no time to celebrate our accomplishments. Seemingly gone are the days when we could slip in a good novel or a catnap on the plane during a business trip, or let our imaginations take off while driving the car. Now cellular phones, pagers, and laptops are our constant, often nagging, companions. When we take vacations, we no longer vacate. Instead, we stay emotionally and literally plugged into work through all our communication gadgets and technology. All of this and more can add up to feeling trapped, overwhelmingly stretched, and being in the dark. Such emotions also weaken our ability to handle change.

"Next week there can't be any crisis. My schedule is already full."
— Henry Kissinger

Like a Creeping Jenny, exhausted and unmotivated employees can gradually shift the organization's work force into one that is dominated by those taking the path of least resistance and working by chance.

Those choked the hardest may totally recoil or become toxic complainers. Besides the inability to handle change well, gone is the ability to innovate and seek solutions. Good people finally depart, taking their knowledge and experience with them because they "can't take it anymore." Organizations where this is allowed to happen will be, at best, mediocre at handling change. More likely, they will not survive.

Our Gift of Choice

So, how do we and the people in our organizations positively create and proactively deal with change? How do we prevent the Creeping Jenny of *living by chance* from overtaking our will to *live by choice?*

> *"We must sail sometimes with the wind and sometimes against it —*
> *but we must sail, and not drift, nor lie at anchor."*
> — Oliver Wendell Holmes

First, let's talk about choice. What is this gift that we humans have over Gracie the Goldfish? I believe it is *our unique ability to initiate or respond in actions and attitudes in ways personal, meaningful and motivating to us.* This ability or gift stays with us even during the most difficult changes — imaginable or unimaginable.

> *"We who lived in concentration camps can remember the men who*
> *walked through the huts comforting others, giving away their last*
> *piece of bread. They may have been few in number, but they*
> *offer sufficient proof that everything can be taken from a man but*
> *one thing: the last of the human freedoms — to choose one's attitude*
> *in any given set of circumstances, to choose one's own way.*
> — Viktor Frankl

Let's talk about some of the misunderstandings and misapplications of our gift of choice. Choice is often confused with control. We know that we cannot control all change, yet how often do we try? We can never fully know or predict new circumstances or situations. But even when we understand that, it is still hard for some of us to relinquish the fact that we cannot control or solve everything.

Sometimes choice is confused with "let others go first." Some of us were socialized to let others choose first. While this is often considered the polite thing to do, it can limit our ability to contribute proactively, build our confidence about making choices, and handle the conflict that may come with our choices.

Our gift of choice is just that; it is ours. But instead of letting it be ours, we make our choices based on what we perceive others or society would want us to choose. We let our choices be outer-directed, not inner-directed.

The essence of this common misunderstanding of "our gift of choice" became clear to me one day as I was reading a study that had analyzed eaters of diet or healthy foods and their motivations for doing so. The study's results showed that there were two groups of people. One group was *inner-directed*. They chose to eat diet or healthy foods because they knew it was good for them. They valued their health and sense of well-being. The second group was *outer-directed*. They chose to eat diet or healthy foods because they wanted to look good to others. In other words, they did it because they valued themselves as they perceived others and society would value them — as healthy and looking good.

Our gift of choice is most effective and fulfilling when it is inner-directed. Our ability to deal with change is enhanced when we make choices that we feel good about, as opposed to choices that we think will be the most accepted or popular with others. If our inner-directed choice turns out to be wrong, instead of giving up, we must choose to learn from it and be proud of having made the choice. Remember, the definition of wisdom is the seasoning gained from a collection of right *and* wrong choices. Outer-directed choices, on the other hand, add to the stress of dealing with change because they leave a nagging pit in our stomach when the choice is not a comfortable fit for us.

One of my favorite stories to further illustrate inner- versus outer-directed choices is one I read about Bonnie Blair. Bonnie was the U.S. speed skater who earned more gold medals than any other U.S. athlete in any winter Olympics, and more than any woman in any Olympic game. Bonnie's ascent to international speed skating acclaim did not begin until she stopped comparing herself to other skaters. By being outer-directed, she pushed herself only to be as good as or better than those she raced. But when she started to race against her personal best, instead of racing against those in the lanes next to hers, she pushed herself to try to beat her own best time each time. By becoming inner-directed, Bonnie became the national and world champion that we came to know.

So how do we find the courage to live by choice, not chance, even when our choice is limited to our attitude and our ability to be inner-directed? How do we find the strength to overcome any weariness, fear, or hesitation we encounter as we struggle to positively create change or proactively deal with it? My suggestion is to more fully recognize and draw upon *grace*.

Our Gift of Grace

Grace is the word I like to use. You can *choose* your own term, but it is your inner strength, inner courage, or inner spirit that enables you to carry through. I believe we all have it. Like choice, it is another gift that only we humans possess.

As I hinted at the start of this chapter, I use *grace* because it has been a meaningful and memorable word to me all my life. Growing up I heard it frequently because it was my grandmother's name. My grandmother personified grace as her fingers glided effortlessly up and down the ivory and ebony keyboard inspiring the inner spirit in others with her music as a concert pianist. Playing tennis as a teenager, I was told by a coach, "You play with such grace." Since then, the word grace has remained special to me, serving as my personal *mantra* for strength and courage. For example, I used it in my corporate career as a calming word, combined with a deep breath whenever I faced a tough meeting or a potentially intimidating person. I even used it as a password on my computer as a daily reminder of inner courage. After this public proclamation, I guess I'll have to find another one.

After holding the word special so long, a few years back I finally looked up *grace* in the dictionary. I found no less than seventeen definitions! These included (1) a prayer before a meal; (2) a title, *your grace*; (3) a favor, to grace someone; and (4) a smooth, gliding action, moving with grace. I liked all of them, but then I found the definition I had been searching for all along. It is the one that can help us deal with change, have the courage to make choices, and develop the resiliency to deal with the results and consequences. Here it is: *grace: the ever-present inner spirit operating in each of us to regenerate and strengthen.* As the definition states, our gift of grace is *ever present* and helps give us the strength to make inner-directed choices and to deal with change.

> *I was always looking outside myself for strength and confidence,*
> *but it comes from within. It is there all the time.*
>
> — Anna Freud

But even if we agree on the definition of this uniquely human gift, it is somewhat abstract, so we will sometimes need practical ideas to help us draw upon it. Here are twelve suggestions. *Choose* what will work best for you at home, at work, and with others with whom you may work, lead, or mentor.

1. Choose to identify your values and priorities.

What are the values and priorities that you do not want to compromise? Once your values and priorities have been firmly established, finding the inner strength to make choices and deal with change becomes much easier. You make the choices or changes that support your values and priorities. Holding steadfastly to what is important to you also makes it much easier to deal with the consequences of your choices, even when unexpected, because of the pride you feel from standing by them. You are making truly inner-directed decisions. Outer-directed choices, on the other hand, dealing with change in ways you believe will be popular with others, may lead to success, but in the long run they will not bring fulfillment. Over time, letting others' opinions or societal "norms" dominate your choices results in what I'll call "succ-stress."

2. Choose to put private time at the top of your "must-do" list.

Set aside time each day to get centered or inner-directed and to reaffirm your values and priorities, if need be. You may accomplish this by sitting quietly, taking a walk, or praying. Let go of current stress. If you're not sure what to think or pray about, just pause to *choose* to reflect upon a positive attitude, such as appreciation. Another idea is to start the day with the snooze button. But instead of using the seven minutes to lie there snoozing, use those precious minutes to get inner-directed, to reflect on possible positive actions, and to choose your attitude for the day before it even starts.

3. Choose to read and participate in things that
  • **support your values and priorities**
  • **foster inner-directed growth and new learning**

Our society constantly bombards us with a variety of messages, many of which challenge what is fundamentally important to us. "Ignorance is bliss" should be changed to "knowledge is bliss" or "continuous learning is bliss." Throughout life, the more we can read about, learn, and participate in things that help us strengthen and define ourselves, the stronger our inner spirit, *grace*, becomes. Read, take classes, or participate in groups to pursue new learning or activities that can provide additional perspective in defining your own self. Add to your knowledge of the arts, history, philosophy, psychology, or religion. If you are a person of faith, pursue your understanding of your religion beyond what you hear "from the pulpit."

4. Choose to keep "tri-healthy."

Without being *physically, mentally,* and *spiritually* healthy and strong, it is very hard to remain inner-directed and live by choice and much easier to slide by, living by chance. Prioritize time to stay healthy. Choosing the first three suggestions already put you well on your way to strengthened mental and spiritual health. And if your quiet time involves walking, you now have all three: mental, spiritual and physical!

> *To keep a lamp burning you have to keep putting oil in it.*
> — Mother Theresa

5. Choose to "try your best" versus "do your best."

Recognize the difference between "trying" and "doing" your best. How often do we hear or tell others "just do you best"? Unfortunately, this message sets up certain failure by setting up the impossible. In every challenge or change in your life, you can *try* your best, but you may not always *do* your best. That means, for example, since my personal best in golf is 85, to do my best every time would mean I would have to "do" 85 every time. Well, the truth is, that was the only time I ever broke 90. But I still "try" my best every time I golf.

Remember the Bonnie Blair story. You may have more potential than you realize, just as she did. Being outer-directed puts too much pressure on us to be the best, and when we figure out we are not the best, (which most of us are not!) it is tempting to lose confidence or blame others, and eventually become comfortable with sliding by on chance. The commitment to try your best every time provides inner pride and satisfaction, no matter the result.

6. Choose to ask for help when you need it.

Our society pressures us to be tough and "have all the answers." If we are outer-directed, we probably won't ask for help. But if you are going through tough times, don't hesitate to ask for help. Find support groups. Think of it as sharing ideas and building on them. And by all means, stay away from toxic "grace-sappers," those individuals who might put undue pressure on you.

If you find yourself uncomfortable about dealing with change, remember this phrase, "If you can't act with grace, leave that place." You may need to leave temporarily, or your inner spirit might tell you to leave permanently. Listen to yourself.

7. Choose to take baby steps.

Even with help, it is sometimes really tough to find the grace and courage to choose the right action or response. Instead of agonizing in indecision or pushing ahead recklessly, put your toe in the water of the situation. Choose to take baby steps, one small step at a time. Soon you will see that those steps (choices) linked together have taken you a long, productive way.

8. Choose to keep a sense of humor.

In any difficult situation, maintaining an appropriate level of levity can be just what you need to get through it. Humor can be in shared dialogue with others, or if you just need some humor for yourself, conjure up fun memories or keep favorite funny pictures or cartoons around. If you are searching for some personal "lightening up," you may want to "do the Mona Lisa." Just try curling the corners of your mouth in that ever so slight Mona Lisa way. You'll be surprised at the positive results. Plus, no one can tell you're doing it, which makes it all the more fun and effective.

If a man insisted always on being serious, and never
allowed himself a bit of fun and relaxation, he would go mad
or become unstable without knowing it.

— Herodotus

9. Choose to realign your perspective.

Put your situation in the context of a bigger picture such as time, the universe, or your priorities. For example, consider how will a difficult change affect you over the years of your life, or even eternity? How does it measure up when looking up at the heavens and the stars? Does it negatively impact any of your values and critical priorities? Time heals, and keeping a larger perspective minimizes the sometimes overwhelming feeling we get in the midst of change.

10. Choose to contain change within its reality box.

It is so easy in our stressed lives to let change or projected negative outcomes become exaggerated in our minds, especially if "toxic grace-sappers" reinforce or create our unreal thoughts and nonsense domino effects. Let molehills remain molehills, and keep mountains from becoming volcanoes — an unsuccessful presentation at work does not mean a lost promotion in the future; an eliminated job does not mean an end to a career, or lost friends or health.

11. Choose to reframe any setback as a possible "spring-forward in disguise."

Almost all of my perceived setbacks have become spring-forwards in my life. For example, a back injury in college curtailed my dreams of professional tennis, but then I was offered a coaching graduate assistantship to pursue an MBA. A health issue forced an end to my corporate career, but then the door opened to start my own company. You may discover the same thing if you take the time to review or journal your setbacks. Did you land in a better place, even though you would never have thought so when the setback took place? Why not take that upbeat attitude from the start? Any time a seemingly negative or "one (or more) step backward" change takes place, choose to believe that in the long run you will be better off and "two (or more!) steps" forward. With that idea as your starting point, the odds are high that you will indeed be better off.

This approach reminds me of a time when a colleague criticized me for having a positive attitude even when things went wrong or turned out differently than expected. I explained my belief that setbacks are often spring-forwards in disguise. His prompt response was something like, "Oh, you're one of those 'cup half-full' people, the kind that sees life through rose-colored glasses. You miss the reality of a situation in which it is necessary to make choices that pragmatically and effectively deal with change." I thought seriously about his comments. Then it hit me. If I truly wore rose-colored glasses in my decision-making, then I would see the glass as two-thirds full or almost full when it was not even close. Instead, choosing a half-full attitude most certainly includes the reality of a glass with the water line at the midway point but with the positive foundation to spring forward.

Searching is half the fun. Life is much more manageable when thought of as a scavenger hunt as opposed to a surprise party."
— Jimmy Buffet

12. Choose to shift your focus away from yourself.

When working through change, get outside of your personal frustrations and moaning and help others who are going through the same change. Beyond assisting that person, you may find that the solutions you offer also help you, or help someone with an entirely different problem or troublesome situation. Help and service to others will help you gain perspective or give you a needed break from your own issues. Whatever you choose to do, as we encourage others, we strengthen our "in-courage."

A Note to Leaders

Understanding and choosing to use our gifts of choice and grace will help us all positively create, and proactively deal with, change. When we are in leadership positions, it is even more important that we use our gifts of choice and grace to the fullest because as leaders we set an example for others through our actions, responses, and attitudes. Choosing to be an inner-directed leader will result in more effective leadership. Picture contemporary and historical leaders as well as leaders whom you have known personally who chose to lead with grace, a visible inner strength, calmness, and command. These are the leaders who successfully rally and inspire their people. These are the leaders who, in the midst of change, attract, unite and motivate others. These are the leaders who not only generate better ideas and solutions, but also inspire others to do the same. These are the leaders who provide order in the midst of chaos and who can maintain the vision above daily grind and short-term crises. These are the leaders who inspire resolve and resiliency in us all.

_____

We can overcome most, if not all, of the weariness, fear, or hesitation that comes with dealing with stress and change by discovering and drawing upon our inner spirit, *grace*. With grace comes the courage to make choices and the resiliency to deal with the consequences. A life that remembers and draws upon the gift of grace and the gift of choice is a fulfilled life. It is a life overflowing with the thrill, pride, and enrichment of lifelong learning and the smiles of gratification that come only with choice, not chance.

Choosing to live with grace is not a fad, a current philosophy, psychology, or model. It is not "ten easy steps" or "six quick fixes." It is not a goldfish. Living and leading with grace is timeless. The gift of choice and the gift of grace are forever ours.

Choose to live with grace.

ABOUT
NANCY HEDRICK, M.B.A.

Nancy Hedrick is President of ReGen Enterprise, LLC, a company she founded in 1999. Nancy works with leaders who want to regenerate their organizations to thrive for the long term through strengthening the strategic positioning of their businesses and equipping their employees to pursue their potential so that they can contribute with greater positive impact to the overall success of the company. Through ReGen Enterprises, Nancy's focus is consulting in the areas of strategic planning and positioning as well as professional speaking with keynotes and workshops in communication, resilience, and leadership. Nancy's approach is grounded in eighteen years in the corporate world of consumer marketing and general management as well as her experience as a national-level tennis player and collegiate coach. She spent ten years at General Mills, where she led such brands as Pop Secret®, Gold Medal® Flour, Bisquick®, and several brands from Betty Crocker® and General Mills cereals. Her last seven years were with ConAgra Frozen Foods where she most recently was Senior Vice President of Marketing, managing close to $2 billion in retail dollar sales of brands that included Healthy Choice®, Marie Callenders®, and Banquet®. Nancy and her teams won many company and industry awards in marketing and advertising.

Contact information:
Nancy Hedrick
ReGen Enterprises, LLC
12811 W. 131st Street
Overland Park, KS 66213
Phone: (913) 814-9504
Fax: (913) 685-7413
E-mail: Nancy@ReGen-Ent.com
Website: www.ReGen-Ent.com

GEAR UP YOUR
ATTITUDE FOR CHANGE

by Chet Marshall

A lost job. A new job. A broken neck. A new arm. A death in the family. The birth of a child. Out with the old management, in with the new. A downturn in the market. Change! This list could go on and on. Alvin Toffler says, "Nothing in this world is more permanent than change."

What "attitude gear" do you usually shift into when these changes occur? Are you in "P"ark, "R"everse, "N"eutral, "D"rive, "L"ow, or "BD"? I'll explain "BD" a little later.

It's inevitable we will experience change throughout our personal lives and careers. These changes are categorized as "forced" changes or "voluntary" changes. The key to success or failure is how we respond. It is our attitude towards the change that increases or maintains our stress levels. These changes demand a high level of adaptability. Wrong responses and attitudes will bring us continual problems. At times our attitudes cause us to create our own barriers to our own possibilities.

Success in "playing the hand that life deals us" depends on our attitude. Price and Prichett say, "To be effective in this new day and age, we've got to know when to give up . . . that is, when to surrender to change. We have to toughen up, in order to develop a higher tolerance for stress. We have to wise up to the ways we're making life more diffi-cult for ourselves. We have too much self-induced stress caused by our mistaken reactions to or attitudes toward change."

The life events mentioned in the first paragraph have happened to me or my friends, and I've had the opportunity to live or observe the attitudes toward each occurrence. The gear shifts from "P"ark to "BD" with one swift motion.

When David, a good friend of mine, was laid off for the third time in ten years, he stood before our church to testify to God's goodness. Each time he has been laid off, the new opportunities that have opened to him offered better positions and more money. As he looked for work, he couldn't wait to see what God had in store for him. He wasn't stressed; he felt peaceful and calm as he sought what was next. His attitude was very positive as he faced this change in his life.

When I saw David at church a few weeks later and asked him how the job search was going, his eyes sparkled, his face glowed, and his smile was broadened as he shared the details of the new position he was to start the next morning. His excitement was overwhelming as he faced this new challenge in his life.

What would be your attitude gear in David's situation?

In June, my wife and I were returning from a church conference in Indianapolis when the cell phone rang. The call was to tell us that one of my wife's sisters had fallen through an artificial ceiling as she was painting. The initial message was that the injury was a broken arm. Later that evening the news from family at the emergency room was that Connie had broken her neck. We dropped what we were doing and rushed to the hospital. Fortunately, the break was not a paralyzing fracture, but she did have severe nerve damage. Connie's attitude was one of thankfulness because there was no paralysis. There's a scripture verse from Ephesians I quote so often in a time of personal tragedy: "In all things, give thanks." We were very thankful because of Connie's attitude.

Connie's life has changed forever. She is still in a neck brace, still experiencing a lot of pain. Her sick-leave days are exhausted, and the job she has had for 21 years has been posted. The prospects of ever being able to return to work are almost nonexistent. She deals with the feeling of being isolated in her country home, unable to do major house-work and relying on others for help while facing additional surgeries.

Connie's attitude, however, is positive in the face of this life-changing event. She is full of gratitude because it could have been so much worse. As she says, "God is good" and "I'm not an invalid, not a vegetable, and I can still maintain a relatively decent life and lifestyle. There are others so much worse off, I'll accept the changes I must." She is playing the hand that life dealt her.

What attitude gear would you be shifting to if you were in Connie's situation?

Ross is a seven-year-old boy, the son of one of our pastors at church. Ross is special to my wife and me as we've been close to his parents for several years. During Ross's gestation period, an amniotic band wrapped around his left arm preventing it's full development. Hence, he was born with a left arm that extends only to his elbow. We've observed firsthand some of what Ross endures because of his handicap. Other kids stare, they question, and he attempts to hide his "little arm" in new environments. However, for a seven-year-old he has managed to have a fairly decent attitude.

He now has a bionic arm, with a hand that can actually pick things up. His excitement with this change in his life is something I wish I could bottle and sell. This new arm isn't like the other kids' arms, but it gives him a sense of normalcy and makes him unique. "Isn't it cool, Chet and Nana, isn't it cool?" Ross says. Yes, it's really cool to watch a small boy deal with change and challenges in a positive way.

What attitude gear would you be shifting to if you were in Ross's situation?

My wife recently lost a very precious aunt. Every Saturday since 1997 my wife and her sisters have been doing what they affectionately called, the "Aunt Irene thing." Aunt Irene went to the "body shop" (beauty shop) to have her copper red hair done every week. One of her nieces would drive out in the country, pick her up, take her to the "body shop," to Kroger's, to Wal-Mart and to Shoney's Restaurant to eat. It was a Saturday ritual that allowed each of them to continue a loving relationship that began when they were small children. She was special and unique — with a crooked smile, a twinkle in her eyes, an unusual sense of humor and an orneriness she thoroughly enjoyed. She was smart, conservative, and loving towards her nieces. She is sorely missed. Her death brought about some changes that required some adjusting.

What attitude gear do you shift into when the death of someone close occurs?

The birth of a child presents new challenges and changes, not only to the parents, but also to grandparents, other family members, and friends. I've often said, "You never know what true love is until you have a child." I quoted that recently to a good friend of mine whose wife had just given birth to a baby boy. The baby was born prematurely and had complications that put him in ICU for several days. A lot of prayers were said in little JAK's (his initials) behalf, and both baby and mother (and father) are doing fine.

His father was describing to me how all of his life's priorities and perspectives had changed when JAK came into the world. There's new meaning to the word "provide," new meaning to the word "parenting," and new meaning to the word "patience." JAK's parents will provide, parent, and have tremendous patience because they know how he fought to stay in their world. The attitude of prayer in gratitude and for guidance will help them to persevere and succeed. Their attitude gears shifted in a very positive way with JAK's arrival.

What attitude gear do you find yourself in when added responsibility comes your way?

Recently, a local bank took out the current management and replaced it with new management from out of state. This bank was the epitome of what personal service was all about. You weren't a number; you were a real person, and the bank employees with whom you conducted business knew you as an individual, knew your name, and knew your character.

Unfortunately, the old leadership of the bank had decided to expand into areas they really knew little or nothing about. "Hey, everybody's doing it, it must be the right thing to do" was the attitude. They bought other banks, property, and businesses and continued delving into things that took their attention away from what it was they did best . . . banking. Financially, the bank suffered a tremendous blow. The board of directors, along with the FDIC, decided that present leadership had to go in order to control the chaos.

The changes that have taken and continue to take place as a result of the change of leadership may be having a positive impact for the stockholders, but they have been very negative for the employees, the customers, and the community. The employees, customers, and community had no control over the changes but had to pay the price for them. The old regime are still getting handsomely paid, but long-time employees are being laid off and power and authority stripped from others, as all the while they are being told to maintain a "positive attitude."

The customers are paying the price through reduced service, increased fees, more complicated process and procedures, and the loss of the personal service they had grown accustomed to. Now all loan decisions are processed through one individual whom the customers do not know and who certainly does not know the customers.

The attitudes concerning this monumental change are all over the gearshift as employees and customers try to make intelligent decisions on how to accept or reject the change. No one knows for sure what the end product will look like, and some are questioning whether or not they want to be around for the end result.

What attitude gear would you find yourself in if you were the customer or employee?

One of the businesses I'm involved in is the aluminum business. We are what the industry calls a "converter," i.e., we do slitting, and we take large coils and make small coils. The aluminum we process is used primarily in the pleasure boat industry and in roofing for semi-truck trailers. Aluminum is a cyclical business, especially in the products we convert. When the economy is good, more pleasure boats are sold.

When the economy is down, truck trailers are used a little longer before replacing them or the roofs.

The last eighteen months we've experienced a tremendous downturn in our business. We're processing only 50 percent of our normal volume. Our profit margins are non-existent and we're having difficulty getting to the break-even point. Regardless of a company's strong financial history, with the economy being down, the banking industry is not as warm and fuzzy as it normally is.

It's been financially difficult for not only me as an owner, but for the other owners and employees as well. Layoffs have us with a bare-bones staff, with no clear picture as to when the market will be back. Getting back to normal is only something we pray for, hope for, and work towards. Surviving in the meantime is the real priority. The market is something we have absolutely no control over. Our business's destiny, for the most part, is in someone else's hands.

The one thing we can control is our attitude with regard to this forced change. There are several gears we could shift to while we're living this change and dealing with its challenges.

What attitude gear would you shift into regarding a change in business climate?

I've continually asked what gear would you be in with regard to the changes we've discussed in this chapter. The gearshift analogy is one I've been using for years when it comes to dealing with change. Some gears are more natural for people than others, depending on individual process. Let's look at the gears in the gearbox and determine which best suits you, depending on the particular change you're engaged in. So, "gear up your attitude for change" as we shift into describing each individual gear.

 First of all, are you in "P"ark, absolutely refusing to budge regardless of what change is taking place? Is your attitude "I've been there, done that, it's time for someone else to take on those responsibilities"?

Or, does your "P" stand for "positive attitude" with regard to change? You realize change is inevitable and you want to participate and not be negative.

 Are you in "R"everse, trying to move yourself so far away that you are of little or no value? Your back-up beeper is loud and clear as you retreat from the challenges facing you.

Or does your "R" stand for "Reliability"? Those around you know they can count on you for support, to be there helping others who may be tempted to retreat.

 Are you in "N"eutral? You haven't really found your place yet. Your responses depend on what group you're talking with at the moment. You're just easily pushed to and fro, not wanting to get on anyone's bad side.

Or, does "neutral" mean you're willing to be flexible in order to make sure everything works to establish a positive environment for change?

 Are you in "D"rive? You're leading the charge to keep things positively flowing towards success in all the challenging changes, both personal and professional. You are not only the driving force, but you take others along for the "drive," influencing them to accept the change in a positive way.

 Are you in "L"ow? It's a struggle, but you're going to keep trudging on, doing the best you can, but at your own slowed-down pace. You're not against change; you just can't mobilize like you used to. Others may pass you by, but you'll get there. Just be patient.

Or, does your "L" mean you're absolutely "lovin' it"? This is an exciting time and you're looking forward to the challenge of change. "Bring it on!" you say.

Are you in "BD"? Let me explain this one. When I was a little boy, somewhere around eleven or twelve, we would visit relatives for vacation. It was the only thing we could afford. We would head to the hills of Kentucky, Carter County to be exact, and I would always stay with my Aunt Clara and Uncle Eck. My thrill was not working in the fields, which I did, but getting the chance to drive "Ole Blue." Ole Blue was an old farm pick-up truck, that even at the age of eleven I couldn't do any damage to. You talk about "been there, done that." Ole Blue had.

But, I can remember it as though it was yesterday: me behind the wheel, my Uncle Eck beside me, my cousins in the back of the truck (at least those who were brave enough), and whatever we were hauling that particular day. We would start up the most difficult road-rutted hill to the house, and I would hear my Uncle Eck in his deepest bass voice say, "Chester, if we're gonna make it up this hill, you better be puttin' her down in "Bull Dog."

So, are you in BD, "Bull Dog"? It's definitely an uphill battle, and you're trying to pull as many as you can with you to the top of "Positive Attitude Hill" and "Power of Influence Summit." Does your "BD" gear stand for "bound and determined" to make the very best of each change and reach the pinnacle of success?

Do you identify with any of these gears when it comes to "forced" or "voluntary" change? Do you use several of these gears, depending on the nature and origin of the change? Are you shifting smoothly from one to the other as the landscape of change occurs? Are you geared up to accept the next challenge of change?

In my very first paragraph I quote Alvin Toffler, "Nothing in this world is more permanent than change." It's a given; every day of our lives we deal with change one way or the other. First recognize that change is imminent, and for the most part we can't control most of the changes that occur, but it is in fact our attitudes that we can control. We decide what gear we are going to shift into.

Another Alvin Toffler quote that I have used often is, "The illiterate of the future are not those who cannot read or write, but those who cannot learn, unlearn and relearn." It's the unlearning that is most difficult. You let go of habits that have worked for you in the past and trade them in for new skills, ideas, and thoughts that will prepare you for the future. With technological changes happening so rapidly, if we find ourselves stuck in "park," we are totally lost in this new technology environment.

We're always hearing that we need to go "back to the basics." The basics will never change, they're our core fiber, but there have been tremendous changes in how we use those basics with regard to attitudes in dealing with personal and professional issues.

Fear is always a factor when we start discussing changes. It probably is the number one cause of resistance to change. I've often said, "We fear most that which we know nothing about." Regardless of what kind of change we're faced with, whether it is in our personal lives or professional lives, the uncertainty of the unknown is terrifying. Fear of change is primarily a result of uncertainty about the unknown, personal insecurity, self-interest, or disruption of the status quo.

Change is a journey, not a destination. We must be willing to maintain a steady movement, shifting gears toward personal and professional goals that will change periodically. Attitude towards change is the key to success, which depends on what attitude gears you've shifted into. Allow this analogy to become a memory hook that will help you in your journey as you "gear up your attitude for change."

ABOUT
CHET MARSHALL

*C**het Marshall is a rare find in the arena of professional speaking. His rich background in the corporate world includes several years in finance, healthcare, manufacturing, retail (as both franchisee and franchiser) and entrepreneurship as a general partner for a venture capital partnership. An experienced CEO in several industries, Chet is an expert on leadership and management, and has spoken on both topics for over 25 years. He is the author of* Lessons on Leadership, Lessons Learned from Bosses on How to be a Boss *and co-author of* Wholehearted Success. *An avid traveler, Chet's speaking career has taken him to all 50 states and most of Canada. A member of the National Speakers Association, Chet's focus is on elevation, overcoming life's challenges, and leadership. His warm and refreshing sense of humor sparks all of his presentations. His characters are very popular. Chet is also active with the Fellowship of Christian Athletes and spends considerable time working with youth, encouraging their growth and success. His zeal for helping others earned him the AAA Meritorious Service Award. If you are looking for powerful, humorous, and meaningful all wrapped up in one creative package, Chet is the right speaker for your event.*

Contact information:
Chet R. Marshall
Elevation Express
130 Summit Ridge
Hurricane, WV 25526
Phone: (304) 545-5100
Fax: (304) 757-5651
E-mail: Chetinwv@aol.com

THE POWER OF A VISION...
A LEADER'S JOURNEY

by Barbara Mintzer

We are living in "interesting times" and these interesting times have brought about a major shift in the values and priorities of today's work force. The unrest in the world and the uncertainty of job security have caused many employees to re-assess their dedication to their jobs. Loyalty to the company has been replaced by the need for stronger ties with family and friends. Managers and supervisors are dealing with the challenge of getting commitment from their employees and helping them feel meaning and purpose in belonging to the company. Motivating employees to buy into the corpo-rate vision, especially during organizational change, would be a good first step in that direction.

Being a leader in business today requires the ability to implement two styles of management. These two styles, used during different stages of organizational change, are **the visionary** and **the coach**. These management styles are far removed from the structured and formal hier-archical style previously implemented in business and are much more appropriate for today's work force.

The visionary accepts the challenge of formulating and articulating a corporate vision that the employees can buy into and work towards. What drives this style are the conviction, passion and enthusiasm the leader has in both the formulation and articulation of this vision. Most employees will not buy into a vision unless they believe in and trust the leader and can feel the leader's own enthusiasm. When organizational change is rampant in a company, and people feel their sense of control and security being taken away, *why should they stay*? What is in it for them in the long run? That is when the visionary comes in. The visionary has the ability to help people see the light at the end of the tunnel . . . and what a great light it is going to be! The visionary can aim big and bring everyone along for the journey, making each person responsible for his or her part in seeing that the vision becomes a reality.

However, before you can formulate a vision for people to follow, you must determine what your values are. Your corporate vision will be a direct reflection of your corporate values. The following is the Values Statement of the Sierra Vista Regional Medical Center in San Luis Obispo, CA.; however, the values expressed in this statement hold true for any industry.

SIERRA VISTA REGIONAL MEDICAL CENTER
VALUES STATEMENT

Demonstrate Respect

We believe each person is a unique expression and therefore inherently valuable.

We believe every encounter is an opportunity to respond to unique individual needs.

We focus on the care we provide to patients, treating them with dignity, respect and compassion.

We acknowledge the unique gifts and diversity of our physicians and employees and seek to integrate those talents in an atmosphere of mutual respect.

We are accountable to the organization, to our patients and to each other.

Foster Integrity

We believe truth and honesty guide our thoughts and our actions at all times.

We are individually responsible for what we do and say.

We build relationships based on trust.

We act ethically in all interactions — there should be no undue influences, conflicts of interest or biased judgments affecting our decision making.

We create an environment that promotes the open and honest exchange of ideas.

Embrace Change

We believe innovation and change must be welcomed and nurtured in order for our organization to increase its capacity to learn and progress.

We encourage the development of a questioning mindset . . . new ways of thinking about everything we do.

We strive to be a learning organization that promotes continuous learning, cultivates creativity and rewards innovation and risk-taking.

We are committed to being flexible and continually responsive to changes in the environment.

We push on the existing boundaries and challenge ourselves to exceed our own expectations and those of others.

Enhance Value

We focus all our efforts on meeting the needs of our patients, physicians, employees, shareholders, communities and others whom we serve.

We ensure quality and cost effectiveness, which are not incompatible, but rather interdependent concepts.

We expect accountability for excellence in performance and for adherence to professional and organizational standards.

We create a work environment that helps people realize their full potential.

We believe economic security for our employees and our physician partners comes from being part of a successful organization.

We bring value to shareholders through effective stewardship of resources, including effective management of corporate expense.

We constantly search for productivity and process improvement consistent with our commitment to quality.

We monitor and evaluate our delivery of care, our business operations and our organizational climate to ensure they meet the needs of those we serve.

We work with others to deliver quality care in our communities and to promote overall community growth and success.

Lead Through Partnership

We lead with our partners to build strategic alliances in order to effectively meet our communities' and nation's healthcare needs.

We recognize that individual, institutional and societal interests are often in tension; we are committed to being an advocate for what is right, recognizing that in every case we must discern how the good of the whole can be served.

We seek to establish mutually beneficial and accountable partnerships based on shared values.

We are dedicated to working for a health system that is accessible and affordable to all.

We join with our physicians and other healthcare organizations to form cost effective care networks focused on quality and responsive to the needs of employers and other purchasers.

The above Values Statement is used with permission of the Sierra Vista Medical Center, San Luis, Obispo, CA. What a terrific values statement it is. Out of it can come your vision statement.

VISION STATEMENT

We are the provider of choice for our products and services.

Customer service is our highest priority, and we are responsive, effective, and innovative in meeting and exceeding our customers' expectations. Our team is knowledgeable, flexible, and accountable for our performance, and we are committed to embracing change. We value those we serve and treat our customers and each other with respect and courtesy. We build relationships based on trust.

That could be your vision statement. It is clear, concise, and has enough content so that every employee can find something he or she could do to bring your vision into fruition. You may want a vision statement that contains more measurable and quantifiable elements. Your vision statement could be: We are the company of choice for our line of products and services, and we realize a 20 percent increase in revenue each year or a 10 percent increase in our client base. However you choose to word your vision statement, you are giving your employees the framework by which they can see themselves involved in making that vision a reality. Once your employees buy into your vision statement, they will immediately start to think about ways they can help you fulfill it.

Why is it so important for leaders and employees alike to have a vision?

Having a vision helps us structure our lives according to our priorities.

We all have such full plates today that it is difficult to know what to do first. However, when you have a vision of what you want to achieve, and you can "taste" what it would be like to achieve it, you start to gravitate to those activities and projects that will lead you closer to your vision. You get that little "quirk" in your heart when you have done something that directly relates to what you are trying to accomplish, and you get that feeling in the pit of your stomach when you are working on something that you know will not lead you where you need to go. The vision we hold becomes the compass that keeps us on track. I find when I am working towards my vision, I somehow still have the time to take care of the day-to-day business that must also get done. It seems my energy level is the highest when I am in gear and motivated to achieve my vision. Many business leaders have told me that a worthy goal or vision is the "fire in the belly" that keeps them going.

Having a vision helps us become failure-resistant.

When I first started speaking, it was a means to get clients for my practice as a career and life-planning specialist. I would speak to any group that asked, usually breakfast and luncheon talks to local clubs and associations in my city. I spoke for two years and never got paid, and at first never thought about speaking as a profession. But I found after two years that I was enjoying the speaking more than the counseling. The dynamics of a group, and being in front of the group motivating many people instead of counseling one, was much more satisfying to me. I had just finished my second year of free speeches when a gentleman asked me to speak for a group he belonged to and asked, "What is your fee?" I almost fainted; I had never heard that before . . . someone thought my speaking was worthy of a fee. While my fee was certainly low (I had no idea what to charge), I WAS A PAID SPEAKER! That fee and the fact that someone paid me to speak gave me the courage and the validity I needed to pursue my career as a professional speaker. From that moment on (19 years ago) *I could not walk into a room without visualizing myself in front of an audience, speaking and having an impact on the lives of the people in my audience.* In those 19 years I have had my ups and downs, my successes and failures, but the vision has never left me. I may make mistakes and fail to live up to my own high expectations of myself, but I am not a failure. I can't allow failure and my vision of me into my life at the same time. As long as I stay true to my vision and work towards it, I know it will keep me failure-resistant.

Having a vision gives us a common bond and purpose to strive for.

One of the most important facets of a vision is the power it has to unify people to strive towards a common goal. When a corporate vision becomes more important than an individual's personal agenda, you rise above the power struggles that can happen at work. Especially during times of organizational change, it is crucial that everyone has a shared vision of what the company seeks to accomplish, and what his or her part is in it.

Having a vision gives purpose and meaning to life.

A vision is the structure that gives life its meaning and purpose. A vision gives us a reason to stretch ourselves, get out of our comfort zones, and try something new . . . a reason not only to embrace change but initiate it. Even though change may be unsettling, if there is something we want to be, do, or have, we will usually bite the bullet and go after it. We learn to look at change as a friend, not as an enemy. A vision allows us a view of what we can aspire to if we are willing to do the work to make it happen.

Many managers and supervisors have told me that, while the above sounds wonderful, they have faced challenges in getting their employees to "buy into" the corporate vision. It has been my experience in working with many companies that, when employees don't buy into a vision, it is because they feel their work would have little impact on the vision, so why bother. They do not feel *accountable* for the vision; that attitude must change. It is the leader's responsibility to make employees accountable for their contribution to the vision.

The following is a *very specific, very powerful* strategy to get buy-in from your employees and make them accountable for the vision. However, this strategy will work only if it is followed exactly as I present it here.

You have now formulated a vision for your employees to work towards. What follows is the **15-minute vision meeting**.

Let us say, hypothetically, that every Friday morning you and your staff meet from 9:00 till 9:15.

Every Friday you meet at the same time, in the same room, everyone takes the same seat, and you always ask the same two questions of your staff:

1. What did you do this week that brought us closer to our vision?

2. What obstacles did you encounter that prevented you from getting us closer to our vision?

That is it! Those two questions never change; they are the same two questions asked week after week, always on the same day (Friday) same time (9:00 to 9:15) in the same room with everyone sitting in the same seat. The power of this strategy lies in the fact that *nothing changes*. It takes about three months for your staff to build a "vision mentality," but after three months that Friday meeting is imbedded in their routine. So now it is Wednesday, and one of your employees is thinking, "Oh boy, it's Wednesday . . . in two days I'm going to be asked those same two questions again; *I had better come up with something to bring us closer to the vision.*" You will be amazed at what that employee will give you.

Managers and supervisors have written to me that they really did not know if the 15-minute vision meeting would work, but they were willing to give it a try. And they have told me what I have just told you . . . after about three months they started to get some of the most creative and innovative ideas from their employees . . . and they said they got some of the best ideas from the people they expected the least of. *Give your employees accountability, and encourage and support their willingness to give you ideas, and they can move your company ahead in quantum leaps.*

Once your employees are actively supporting your corporate vision and working towards making it a reality, the management style of *coaching* is the most effective way you can sustain employee productivity and effectiveness. This hands-on, one-of-the-team style of management provides a climate of trust that is conducive to keeping employees motivated and engaged in their work. There are four key qualities to effective coaching:

1. Loyalty: Employees today do not feel much loyalty from management. They have seen family and friends go through layoffs, and they come into the workplace with a self-protective attitude. It is imperative that management show loyalty to employees for a coaching relationship to work. While companies may no longer be able to guarantee "forever" employment, coaches can show loyalty to their employees in a number of ways:

- Honest communication . . . give timely and reliable information to your employees . . . always important, and especially so when an organization is going through change. If they trust you and respect you and know you are being honest with them, they will be able to handle the information, even if it is not positive. Most employees will give everything they have to help you turn the situation around, if they feel included.

- Allow employees to express how they feel without fear of punishment or retribution . . . a must if you want to build trust and loyalty with your staff.

- Never ask employees to do something that goes against company ethics or values.

- Encourage employees to grow and develop their potential, and support them in their endeavors. Be grateful for the risk-takers in your organization; it's their creativity and innovative thinking that will keep your company competitive. Encourage and support risk-taking, provided the ideas and actions are thought-out beforehand and are not reckless.

- Treat each employee as a *unique* individual. Everyone wants to be appreciated and acknowledged for his or her own special attributes. Get to know your employees better so you know their frustrations as well as their aspirations. The most effective coach is the one who is truly "tuned in" to the players on his or her team.

2. Empathetic Listening: One of the most undervalued of all management skills is the ability to listen. A coach often spends more time listening than managing. When an employee needs to be heard, the coach:

- Finds a private spot (a neutral place like the cafeteria off-hours if the employee is likely to feel intimidated in the coach's office) and makes time available to listen.

- Holds all calls unless urgent and lets the employee know that there will be no interruptions. The employee has all the coach's time for (x) amount of minutes. We spend time with things we value, and this non-interrupted time is a strong signal to the employee that he or she is important and valued.

- Sits down and leans forward in an "I am interested" position and focuses on what the employee is saying, sometimes taking notes if appropriate.

- Asks open-ended questions to draw the employee out and pays close attention to what is said. Try asking questions such as: What are your persistent frustrations? What do you need to perform your job that has not been provided? What would the ideal job in this company look like for you? In the answers to these questions, you discover what is at the heart of the problem, and your employee will feel understood when his or her needs and concerns can be accurately verbalized by the coach.

- Lets the employee know that the coach is in his or her corner and willing to help. "How can *we* work through this" is an excellent phrase for showing empathy and concern.

3. Skills Stretching: To run a team that is competitive, creative, and innovative, the coach should create an environment in which employees are given an opportunity to develop new skills. Creative and innovative employees love to be challenged in their work and to grow in new skill development. The coach should carefully evaluate the strengths, weaknesses, and confidence levels of each employee, and move individuals into areas where their skills can be expanded and their interests can be developed. Classes and seminars can be effective tools in achieving skills-stretching. However, sometimes all it takes to develop potential is added responsibility and encouragement along the way.

4. Role Modeling: Coaches are role models whether they know it or not. The staff members' view of the coach can affect their attitude towards the entire organization. How each staff member feels about the coach can have a profound effect on how productive he or she is. Coaches can be excellent role models by:

- Providing a "level playing field." The coach does not show favoritism, and each employee is judged equally on his or her work performance.

- Giving employees constant and consistent feedback on their performance.

- Showing appreciation for employees. When coaches give employees approval, praise, and recognition when it is due, employees respond by becoming more committed to the company and to its vision.

- Taking pride in themselves and their own work and modeling the behavior that they would require of their employees.

Coaching is not easy. But the reward is great . . . a cohesive, alive, "excited about the future" team, working together towards a shared vision. It is this type of team that will keep a company competitive and on top in the rapidly changing work place.

ABOUT
BARBARA MINTZER

*B*arbara Mintzer is an internationally recognized, award-winning speaker and consultant with over 30 years in business and health care. She was one of the first women in the United States to sell wholesale pharmaceuticals for a major drug company. Her ability to create selling opportunities where none previously existed earned her numerous honors, including a cover story in the American Druggist Magazine. After success-fully moving up into management, Barbara moved on, and in 1982, formed her own consulting and training company. Barbara specializes in assisting organizations, teams and individuals to create tomorrow's opportunities out of today's changes. More than 200,000 business and health care pro-fessionals across the United States, Canada, England, Australia and Brazil have benefited from her inspiring message.

Contact information:
Barbara Mintzer
B.A. Mintzer & Associates
4019A Otono Drive
Santa Barbara, CA 93110
Phone: (800) 845-3211
Phone: (805) 964-7546
Fax: (805) 964-9636
E-mail: BMintzer@west.net
Website: www.BarbaraMintzer.com

EMPOWERMENT:
USE IT OR LOSE IT

by Jasun Light

Y ou are magnificent! You are powerful! These were the words
that my personal trainer, Dennis Croll, had drummed into my
head repeatedly while we practiced running hills in the early
dawn hours just before sunrise. He was preparing me for the greatest
adventure I had ever undertaken, running a marathon along the lush
green rain forests and beautiful, golden, sandy beaches of New Zealand's
South Island. For over nine months I had daily trained and prepared for
this event. And then the day came. I ran through some of the most spec-
tacular scenery in the world, and I completed the race. In the process, I
learned a few things along the way about empowering others and myself.

You see, for me life is just like a marathon; it takes time to prepare,
to practice, and then to complete the event. And if you want to complete
it successfully, then you have to be prepared to put in the time and to
dedicate yourself, with full commitment and daily discipline, to make it
happen. A marathon is long, takes enormous amounts of physical
training, and success is not guaranteed. But real winners, who complete
the race successfully, do so because of their emotional training and their
mental fitness.

During the race through the rain forests and shorelines of New
Zealand, I came across an athlete who was 21 years old, in the peak of
her life, strong and powerful, graceful as a gazelle, and able to cross
running streams in a single stride. She was beautiful to watch, as she

passed me by and left me in her shadow. Much later on, I caught up with her at a drink station, where she sat holding her head in her hands, crying and sobbing. Her friends were there to support her, but she just kept saying to herself and them, "I can't do it! It's too hard. It's just too difficult! I just can't do it!"

I learned at the finish that she never did finish the race. Clearly she was in the prime of her life physically. She was just as strong and powerful as anyone else there. But emotionally she had not yet developed the mental endurance necessary to complete the event. At the finish, a 55-year-old man, clearly past his prime, crossed the finish in a time of 3 hours and 40 minutes. Amazing. It made me wonder. How could a 55-year-old defeat a 21-year-old?

Empowerment Rule #1 —
Power is a State of Consciousness; Powerful Self-Talk and a Powerful Self-Image Create Success.

I got a flash of sudden realization. Success is not determined by outside factors. Success is your own state of consciousness. Physical fitness and success, whether running a marathon or running your life, is not so much a skill of physical endurance but of emotional training. Maturity is not a physical state but a mental state, characterized by a strong belief in yourself. The older man clearly had more experience, more self-knowledge of his abilities, and more confidence in his own performance. He was self-empowered. The young woman had youth, vitality, energy, and excitement on her side but lacked the self-empowerment that she so desperately needed. Her self-defeating thinking controlled her mind, and stopped her from going on, even though her body was perfectly capable.

I quickly took stock of my own situation. I was about two thirds of the way through the 26.2 miles of this marathon. I still had at least maybe eight or nine miles to go. I was tired, exhausted, and hurting, but I also wasn't going to stop. I knew my body well enough to know that if I slowed down, I would start to let those very same doubts that plagued the young female athlete into my mind, and I would end up just like her.

Right then and there, I made this decision: "I believe in myself, I believe in my capabilities, and I know that I can finish the race." The goal, the finish line, was still a long way away, so I started to program my mind and my heart to keep going. I told myself, "I know that if I just focus and concentrate on relaxing, breathing deeply, staying on track, and pacing myself, I can make it. I just need to stay loose, enjoy the awesome scenery, be in the moment, have fun, and keep moving steadily. I will make it."

I learned from Dennis, a veteran of extreme endurance races, that the key is to visualize the finish line, while focusing your primary attention, on the path in front of you. If you don't, your mind gets overwhelmed with the task ahead, the incredible distance to go, and you quickly become demoralized. The real trick for a big undertaking like a marathon (or any other big challenge you may be facing in life), is to have the vision of the finish line in the back of your mind, yet have your whole awareness preoccupied with where you are right now in the present moment. You must keep your attention squarely on the ground, directly in front of you, looking precisely where you place each step, concentrating exactly on the task at hand, making each stride cover the maximum distance. I did just that. I chanted to myself positive affirmations to keep me emotionally enthusiastic, even though my body was physically under stress. "I can do it! I can do it! I can do it! Do it now!"

So I learned something. Self-talk, how you talk to yourself on a daily basis, has an enormous impact on how you will perform during an ordinary day or during a race. In this instance, it was the race that made the young woman's thoughts visible to herself and to all around her. Normally, we are not in such stressful situations that we display our inner thoughts to public view. But ask yourself this: "How often do I let negative, self-defeating, or self-doubting thoughts into my head?" If you do, then get control of them immediately. Nip them in the bud, fast, right away. Anchor yourself in a peak performance state of mind.

Anchoring yourself in a peak performance state of mind requires you to use the power of your mind to put yourself in a powerful state of life mastery. For example, you face a challenge, something that requires strength and endurance, such as starting your own business. First, know that you can do it; you just need to get in shape, prepare, practice, and follow through. Get yourself in top physical and mental fitness, and the confidence that you are as fit as can be will give you the emotional power to know that you can be successful. You can do it! Give yourself permission to accept your power, use your power, and use your freedom to succeed. Our success is largely determined by our own belief in ourselves.

Empowerment Rule #2 —
Our Own Belief Systems About Ourselves
Govern Our Behavior and the Results We Achieve.

Our thoughts are the very foundation from which our energy emanates. Our thoughts are more in control of our lives than we are presently aware. The core issue is not "how to become powerful"; we already are powerful! Being powerful is our natural state! We are born with enormous power already within us!

The real question is why do we delude ourselves into thinking that we are not powerful? Why do we deny our own power, and act shy and passive, when deep inside of us is an enormous well of creative energy just waiting to burst forth, if we would only allow it. Why do we not believe in ourselves and our power and behave assertively enough to let the power come out and manifest itself in reality?

Unfortunately we often sabotage our efforts and put ourselves in a mental prison of self-doubts. These doubts are usually the leftover intentions of our parents, teachers, and authority figures, who wanted to warn us of the dangers of life. They meant well, trying to protect us from harm from the outside world, but they inadvertently planted within us the seeds of self-doubt; the self-doubts they themselves had harbored for so long. Since most of our peers and associates have also been subjected to this phenomenon, they also harbor many self-doubts. Our peers and their belief systems are probably one of the most influential forces shaping our lives.

Whom you associate with on a regular basis has an enormous

impact on what you believe to be true about yourself, and what you believe you can achieve. These belief systems determine our conduct from day to day and the results we accomplish, in a year, a decade, or a lifetime.

We have a fantastic, dynamic creative energy within us already; it just needs to be reawakened and allowed to manifest itself. I am a believer in the principle, "You can do anything in the whole world, if you just put your mind to it!" All we really need to do is give ourselves the freedom to be ourselves and love who we are.

Empowerment Rule #3 —
Powerful Internal Feelings of Success
Create a Self-Fulfilling Prophecy in our External Life.

Life is a self-fulfilling prophecy. If we think about success, act successful, expect success, practice success, we will be successful. But, unfortunately, the opposite is also true. If we sow the seeds of doubt, we reap the consequences of doubt. If we are going to think, we might as well think of success and prosperity all the time. This internal programming will certainly manifest itself in our daily life. Think powerful. Believe powerful. Act powerful. Be powerful.

Before I completed the New Zealand marathon, I was an out-of-shape, fat, bald, middle-aged guy, with a sedentary lifestyle, sitting in front of a computer for hours a day. Who would have ever thought that I could get myself motivated and in shape to run a marathon? Not me, that's for sure. But that's exactly my point. For ten years I had programmed myself to think of myself as just another person who sits at a desk. Was I the kind of person to be a supreme athlete? I didn't think so. Fortunately I was smart enough to realize that those were assumptions that I was making about myself. Nobody else was putting these labels on me, except me. And then the inspiration dawned on me: "The only limits on me, are the limits I put on myself.' If you meditate on this thought, it will give you a great insight into your life and liberate you to explore new horizons, and discover success you never even dreamed possible before. Let go of your limitations and create your life.

The process of creating your life starts with your thoughts. Thoughts repeated over and over become ingrained, core beliefs and the foundation from where we operate in the world. You become what you believe to be true about yourself. Since we all have beliefs about who we are, and what we can accomplish in our lifetime, we might as well believe big, bold, powerful thoughts of strength, achievement, and success. Believe in yourself and in your natural ability to succeed. Believe in yourself! I did, and you can too.

Empowerment Rule # 4 —
The Quality and Quantity of our Power is Directly Proportional to our Willingness to Take 100% Responsibility for our Lives.

It really all comes down to us; how much we are willing to assume accountability for our lives. The closer we are to taking 100 percent responsibility for our lives, the more we realize that success is not due to external forces but to our own level of development and expertise. We place success squarely on our own shoulders and realize that our success is up to us. If we don't make ourselves successful, who else do we think is going to do it for us? We have an internal locus of control. We are in control of our life, we are in control of our destiny, and what we make of our life is our own responsibility. The more self-mastery we exhibit the more personal freedom we will enjoy. How much are we willing to hold ourselves accountable?

When I was two-thirds through the marathon and enduring the physical stress of the event, I accepted that nobody could help me reach the finish; I had to do it on my own. My personal trainer, Dennis, had prepared me, but he wasn't there at the moment. If I was going to get to the finish, it was up to me. It was my responsibility. It was my adventure, and I had a responsibility to carry myself through to the end. Then I discovered something amazing. As I passed other people along the way, I smiled, gave them a word of encouragement, and told them confidently, "You can do it!" Helping others feel confident in their own abilities reinforces your own belief in yourself. Every time I lifted someone else's spirits, I simultaneously lifted my own.

Real winners in life look at themselves objectively, honestly, candidly, and without getting emotionally attached to their predicament. They calmly, yet self-assuredly, create a strategy to solve their problems. Real empowered people do not wait for things to happen to them. Real empowered people are proactive and go out into life and make things happen for themselves and others. The more we can find ways to benefit other people, the more other people will find ways to benefit us. The best way we can empower others is to become powerful ourselves. We lead by example.

Empowerment Rule #5 —
One of the Most Powerful Things You Can Do is Make Yourself an Integral Part of a Mastermind Network of High Achievers.

I am a very strong believer in teamwork, and in working closely with other people with the same drives and ambitions. Having a mastermind network, of other focused and fast-paced people is one of the best ways to assure your success. Power comes from within yourself, but it is magnified if given the opportunity to operate in a team environment with similar people focused on a vision, ambitious to reach their goals, and driven by determination to succeed.

One thing I know for sure. There is no way I would have ever been able to do that marathon if I had not had the help of Dennis. He pulled me through the tough conditioning runs, up and down the hills, and over the miles of trails we traveled. Training at sunrise, we would run watching the sun give birth to a new day. And we celebrated life as we ran! He taught me about enjoying the process of transformation from desk potato to marathon runner. He believed in me when I didn't even think it was possible for me to believe in myself. He pushed me hard when I didn't think I could go on but he knew I could. He taught me to do more, and be more, than I thought I ever could before. That is what friends are for. And for that I owe him more than words can convey. With teamwork, you can accomplish and achieve more than you can even imagine. Believe me; I know from personal experience.

Synergy is produced when people with a common purpose devote all their energy to a particular cause. That energy is enthusiasm, and it becomes contagious to all who encounter it. Within a team, your own power increases exponentially, and you are able to do things you never thought possible before. Team synergy is a successful tool many people use to reach peak power, whether at a championship sports event, an important business project, climbing Mount Everest, or even running a marathon. Teams allow individual persons to go further than they possibly thought they could go on their own. Get on a peak power team in your career, and if you can't find one, then create one! Be a leader.

Empowerment Rule #6 —
Real Authentic Power Comes from Trusting Yourself,
Exercising Your Power Daily, and then
Putting Yourself in a Creative Leadership Position.

Being powerful is something anyone can do; it just takes self-discipline, love, and patience. Exercise your power, every day. Power is just like going to the gym. If you want a really fit body, you have to exercise every day. And a fit body is the result of loving your body, and giving it the discipline and time it needs to accomplish what you want. Power is exactly the same; you need to exercise it every day, to build it up and make it strong. Find a way to exercise your power every day.

When we are strong and ready, we need to be a role model to others and mentor them in developing their own power. We need to find opportunities where we can play a leadership role in society. We need to take our creative energy, give it out, and show the world. Be willing to be an inventor: to do what has never been done before. Be a leader. Be a player in life.

Why did I choose to run a marathon? What's the point? Was I just going through that midlife crisis? No, it was something more profound. I discovered that life is boring if you just resign yourself to living within your comfort zone. And I had been comfortable way too long. It was then I figured it out. Life is not about getting comfortable, not for me anyway. Life is about reaching out to try new challenges, and about being willing to really stretch myself to accept new roles and create new definitions of myself and what I am capable of. Why not create a new role for myself, marathon runner? Why? Because it is something I had never done before. And it was time to leave my comfort zone, spread my wings, and see if I really could fly. And I did.

The world is full of dreamers, idealists, and people with a lot of good intentions. But they also spend most of their time sitting in the audience, watching someone else do all the action on the stage of life. If you want to be an empowered person, start looking at ways in which you can place yourself on the center stage of your life, and invite other people to come to watch you perform. Get out of the audience of mediocrity, and join the empowered people who are on the center stage of life. Stop being a spectator. Be a player. Be a star. Create your role, invent your place in society, and then live it. We are not stagnant nouns; we are living, dynamic, verbs. Make your life a living masterpiece.

When are we going to wake up to the enormous power that lies within us? When are we going to stop pretending that it doesn't exist? When do we actually utilize it for the benefit of ourselves and everyone around us? Show the whole world how powerful you are! What are you waiting for? In actuality, it is your obligation and your duty to use your power, to be successful. Your failure helps neither you nor anyone else around you. But your power and your success help you and everyone around you. Know your power. Use your power. Demonstrate your power. Be a powerful force in the world; you owe it to yourself, to your family, and to everyone you know.

How can we make ourselves more powerful? By realizing that being personally powerful is possible. By identifying fears, and then systematically eliminating those fears by doing precisely that which we are afraid to do. By doing exactly what we fear to do, we teach ourselves to be powerful. Set a new standard for yourself by refusing to be held hostage by your fears any longer. Create a personal code of conduct that stipulates from this moment on, you will act powerful and you will be courageous at every opportunity. Make a life decision to be powerful. Be adventurous, and give your heart to love. You need to recognize that the opposites of fear are the emotions of courage, bravery, and love. Find ways to consciously and confidently exercise your courage and love. Be daring in your actions.

Be bold, be brave, and have faith that you are going to succeed. Focus on being more loving in the world. Do little things at first, start out small, and work your way upwards. Find ways to show love for yourself, love for your family, love for others around you. Love is the answer. When our love builds enough it becomes so abundant that it overflows and we cannot contain it any longer. We will want to share our love with a wider circle of influence. We become the persons that make positive things happen. We become the leaders, and people recognize us.

There are no limitations! The only limitations we have are the ones we place on ourselves! We live in the greatest civilization on Earth. We have a standard of living far surpassing any other time in history. We have a constitution and a political system that favors personal freedoms and individual rights. We have access to resources that are probably available to only 10 percent of the people living in the world today. We have the most opportunities, and we are the most fortunate, the most privileged, group of people, of all time. We are the chosen ones.

Never in all of history has there ever been something as wonderful and awe inspiring as America is today. It really is the land of abundance, the land of opportunity. All you need is to shift your state of consciousness from fear to love. Shift from scarcity to prosperity. Shift from pessimism to optimism. Shift from being a spectator to being a leader. Shift from passive to proactive, assertive control. Shift from being normal to being tremendously powerful.

Empowerment Rule #7 —
Genuine Strength and Power come from High Levels of Self-Esteem and Self-Confidence. Power comes from our Love of our Life.

Real self-empowering comes from high levels of self-confidence and high levels of self-esteem. Over and over again studies have shown that people do not lack knowledge. The world is full of college graduates who are only drifting through life, without really applying themselves, without harnessing their own abilities. You know people like that. I do. Is it that they aren't smart or intelligent? Of course not. In my opinion, they lack that vital quality which isn't taught at universities or graduate school. It is called developing a high level of self-esteem, high self-confidence, and superior communication skills. These are the most important tools we need to be successful in our modern world.

With high self-esteem, and high self-confidence, you feel that you can take on any challenge that the world gives you. Without these, you simply are not functioning at your optimum level. The people without these skills wonder what is wrong with them and why they aren't getting ahead. You get the picture. Self-esteem and self-confidence, and the ability to communicate, are essential skills, which many people have, and they are usually the ones who make the most money. The fact is, these vital skills are the foundations of success. If you don't have them yet, get started on a program to acquire them as soon as you can.

This is one area I can not emphasize enough: Love yourself. All great success starts with a deep love of oneself. Training for a marathon, there were many days when I simply didn't have the heart to go out for my daily runs. But then I learned something else. The physical pain of hard, strenuous exercise was counterbalanced with great feelings of self-esteem and self-confidence once I was finished. Soon, getting out of bed at 5:00 am wasn't something I had to force myself to do with willpower; it was something I was so excited about because I knew that the physical pain was temporary, only an hour or so, but the self-esteem, and the accompanying self-confidence, were benefits which would last throughout my lifetime. And you can't even put a price on how valuable that is. Life is so precious! Self-love is everything. With it, anything is possible, and without it, you are lost in limbo.

Empowerment Rule #8 —
True Empowerment Emanates from Our Love
for our Physical and Emotional Well-Being.

Which brings me to the last point of being empowered. Power is one word, self-love. And one of the best ways to love yourself is to exercise! Make exercise the most important, the most vital, enthusiastic, part of your day. Exercise is the elixir of life! Exercise is the fountain of youth! (Just watch any five-year-old run around all day long, never giving a thought to anything but sheer exuberance and fun.) Exercise is one of the most wonderful ways that we can spend our time. Exercise also extends our time. The more we exercise, the better our overall health and fitness, the longer we will live. The more exercise, the more we feel in control of our life. The stronger our physical body gets, the more we feel the strength to cope with challenges in other areas of our life. Physical power and physical strength have a direct and positive connection with the mental power and emotional power and social aspects of our lives.

Remember the 55-year-old marathon runner? What made him finish so strong? I personally believe it was the mental and emotional endurance he had developed. Maybe call it self-mastery; one thing is for sure, when we have it, we can far surpass any of our previous accomplishments. When I was nearing the finish of my epic run, I knew that I had done something that I had never done before. And that sense of achieving a personal best record, for myself, is a wonderful feeling which has to be experienced. For you, it may be another challenge such as creating a business opportunity, and putting all your business acumen and skills to the test to come out a winner.

Being in an athletic mode of living frees our body to explore new realms of possibility. When we exercise we often do it as recreation. Or if we see it for what it really is: re-creation. Each time we exercise we literally re-create ourselves. And creating your life, just as you want it to be, is what empowerment is all about. If you had unlimited power to create your life just as you wanted it, what would it be like? And what type of excuses are you using to keep you from having that type of lifestyle? What is your pay-off for your procrastination? Exercise lets us tap into that creative force within us, the driving force of success in our daily lives. Say yes to being a creative force. Make your life a masterpiece.

Now does this mean being eccentric and training for the

Olympics? No. But it does mean that you do your everyday activities in an athletic way. Sprint to your mail box, just for fun; maybe there is a love letter in the mail box. Be an athlete in the bedroom. Be an athlete whether you are mowing the lawn, or dancing at a cocktail party. Be an athlete when you go to a hot tub, or a swimming pool. Imagine disrobing and having the eyes of the bystanders stare at your awesome body in your sexy swimsuit. That is empowerment.

Be an athlete in ways you never imagined. How about running a marathon? Maybe that is too much too soon? O.K., but don't doubt it either. Anything is possible. You can do anything in the world, if you just put your mind to it. Let yourself go. Let yourself be powerful. Let yourself use your power; let yourself demonstrate your power! In fact, it is your responsibility to be successful! The more powerful you are, the more you will attract others to you. The more powerful you are, the more people will admire your dignity and the respect you have for yourself. The more powerful you are, the more you are able to help your family and your friends. Your power has the ability to affect many lives. It is your responsibility to be powerful.

Exercise your power daily. Make a decision, right now, that you are the one who will make a difference. Decide that you will use your power for the benefit of all that you meet. If you do that over a long enough time, you will find that empowerment won't be something you have to read about in a book. Empowerment won't be something you do. Empowerment won't be something you feel. Empowerment won't be something that you practice. Empowerment will be something *you are*! And when that day comes, you will know it! Because you will experience something from deep within you, your spirit, your voice, saying, "You are magnificent! You are powerful!"

ABOUT
JASUN LIGHT

Jasun Light communicates energy, empowerment, and enthusiasm. A "BrainPower" expert, Jasun's specialty is encouraging audience members to explore the vast untapped BrainPower which each of us possesses, but which few of us know how to develop to optimum performance. Our society is right in the midst of an enormous shift into the information age, where human intelligence and character are the most valuable assets of any corporation. The most successful people of the future will be those who know how to access and communicate the most of their dynamic, creative, intellectual capital. Call on Jasun to custom create an opportunity for your team to discover their leading edge, their ability to build a Mastermind network, and exponentially utilize their awesome BrainPower. A native of Tucson, Arizona, Jasun has an honors degree in Psychology from the University of Arizona. His more popular presentations include: "You are a Genius!," "Keep Going, Keep Growing!," and "Create Success!" A husband, father, and community leader, his next challenges include writing books and training for marathons.

Contact information:
Jasun Light
BrainPower
P.O. Box 65478
Tucson, AZ 85728-5478
Phone: (520) 299-9999
E-mail: JasunLight@earthlink.net

The Domino Principle of Dealing With Change

by Mark Hunter

We notice change when it occurs abruptly. We rarely see change when it affects us slowly.

To help understand this idea, let's look at a couple of examples. Remember what it felt like on the first day of a new job? Remember how much change you felt that you were experiencing? Or how about the change you went through the day you sold your worn out, 10-year-old car with bald tires and suddenly began driving the new car you had always dreamed of owning? It's easy to see big change; however, we don't notice change when it occurs slowly in our lives. We didn't pay much attention to the tread on the tires of the 10-year-old car each day when we drove it. But one day we noticed how bald the tires had become when we tried to stop suddenly. You see, in our lives, change occurs daily, yet only when significant things occur do we pay attention to the changes occurring around us.

For us to understand how to deal with change and, more importantly, how we can actually use change to our advantage, we have to acknowledge and accept that change is occurring all around us each day. We usually pay more attention to significant changes, but, because of the sudden change, we often find ourselves in a defensive or reactionary mode. This type of response is not abnormal, and it is not unusual, considering we generally strive for a level of consistency and balance in our lives. The fact we may become reactionary in our response to change is not always bad; in fact, it's actually quite good that we condition ourselves to be able to handle the impact of change, both good and bad, in an appropriate manner. When we can react to change in a way that does not cause us to lose focus or composure, we are in control. Naturally, then, it is this type of person who is perceived as a leader and one whom people will naturally gravitate toward in times of change.

Even more important than dealing with major change is the need for us to be aware of changes that are occurring daily in our environment and our lives. For it is the daily changes, however slight, that result in the bigger changes that catch our attention. Therefore, the best way for us to thrive in the midst of change is to be aware of change as it occurs daily.

The best way to describe the daily impact of change is by thinking of a set of dominoes all standing on end in a long row. Should any single domino fall, it would be of no consequence. But, because the dominoes are all in a row, when one falls, it automatically has an effect on the next one, which in turn affects the next one, and so on, until they've all fallen over. Think of a single domino as the change that occurs in your life each day, and you can begin to see a picture of the impact that daily change makes over a period of time. When we begin to look at the individual elements of significant changes in our lives, we usually see that the major change was really a result of numerous smaller changes that we failed to pay attention to, occurring over a much longer period of time.

By looking at change on a daily basis, we begin to see how we can influence the impact of change, and, more importantly, how we can influence change by being *ahead* of it rather than behind it. In today's environment, our actions at work, in the community, and even in the world, are intermingled. Therefore, if we are going to thrive when change is going on all around us, we need to be in tune with the little changes that are occurring daily.

In the workplace, in order for us to see change and to thrive in its midst, we have to develop skills that allow us to notice change. But just being able to notice the change is not good enough. If we are to lead in the workplace, we must also be in a position to influence the change.

The difference between seeing change and influencing change is similar to the difference between watching a climber on the face of a mountain and being the climber. To the person who is watching the mountain climber, the focus is on the distance traveled. For the person climbing, the focus is on where the next step is going to be and how that next step will set up the next step. A mountain climber knows that each step is not taken independently; rather, each step is based on the results of the previous step, designed to successfully allow the next step to occur. As a leader, we need to view every day in the same light that the mountain climber views each step of a climb. We must realize and look for the impact that each activity or event has on subsequent activities or events.

To help us to see and influence change, we should continuously ask ourselves the following questions:

1. What do we do as a business that drains resources from our company or department? (An example might be a particular service, a process, an activity, or even a particular customer.)

2. Do we know the true cost, in time and money, of each activity that we perform as a company or department?

3. What questions are new employees asking, and what can we learn from them?

4. What would change if someone else came in to do my job?

When we use these questions as a prompter, we can begin to observe change and to understand how we might influence it and thrive in its midst. Looking more closely at each of the four questions, we can see how they can be applied in our workplaces on an on-going basis.

First, *what do we do as a business that drains resources from our company or department?* The key to answering this question is to review elements such as processes, services, activities, and even customers. Nothing you do is so small that it should be overlooked. This question is a direct response to the habit we all have of doing things today because we did them yesterday, never stopping to ask ourselves why we're even doing them in the first place. When we do things the same way continuously, we fail to spot changes that are occurring ever so slightly, changes that, over time, compound to make the things we are doing unrealistic. Then we find ourselves scrambling to alter a process, find a new customer, or change an entire department when the change that has been "ever so slight over time" becomes overwhelming. If we had been noticing all along the situations and events that drain our resources, we would have been in a better position to deal with the change before it became so overwhelming.

The challenge in answering this question lies in breaking down tasks into small enough details that we can see them clearly. Again, an example helps to explain this process. If we stand on the edge of a forest, we might see how lush and green everything is. We will probably be in awe of how so many different types of vegetation can come together to make such a peaceful setting. Only when we actually enter the forest are we able to see the withering plants, the diseased trees, or the insects devouring critical parts of the vegetation. Because we have now taken the time to enter the forest and view items individually, we're now able to see how many issues need to be dealt with to keep the forest lush and green. If we had chosen to view the forest only from a distance, we would never have spotted the problems until it was too late. By going into the forest, not only do we see the disease and problems, but we learn first-hand how to deal with them.

In the example of a forest, the changes — and problems — are fairly easy to see. The trick is seeing the same amount of detail in the workplace, because rarely does change present itself so vividly as a diseased tree or a withering plant. Therefore, it is important for us to break apart each element, each task, and each activity within our businesses to really understand what has changed. When we go through this process, we will begin to see more easily what is changing and what is not working because of those changes. By adapting to changes when they are small, we have far more ability to influence the change, putting us ahead of it rather than behind it.

We break apart these tasks and activities by interacting with the people involved, by benchmarking the process, and by setting up a procedure whereby the activity we are evaluating can be viewed differently. Don't settle for the easy conclusion that if it's not broken, you shouldn't touch it. More times than not, that type of response is a scapegoat for laziness — it's our way of convincing ourselves that, when things do get out of control, we'll be able to handle them. By taking this approach and not taking the time to examine things more closely, we miss the real opportunities that are lurking just underneath the surface.

Second, *do we know the true cost, in time and money, of each activity that we perform as a company or department?* On the surface, it may appear that this question is just another way of stating the first question. In a way, this is true. The real benefit in asking this question lies in preparing us for our response to change. By understanding what each task or activity costs in its truest sense, we're in a position to make more intelligent decisions when we do see changes occurring. Often, when we first see changes occurring, we spend much of our time trying to determine the likely impact on us, and then we begin to determine what we need to change. The problem with this reaction is very simple: it takes too much time. In fact, we can spend so much time answering these questions that, by the time we are finally able to make a decision, even more change has occurred, and we find ourselves even farther behind. By evaluating *up front* what the true cost in time and money is for each task or activity, we can respond much faster to change when it occurs.

Another problem that this question helps us avoid is the tendency to express a "knee-jerk" reaction in response to a change that must be dealt with quickly. We've all been in these types of situations — the ones that arise so quickly that we are blind-sided by issues that could have a profound impact on us. A rapid change allows us no time to do anything but react and hope that our gut instinct and our knowledge will guide us in making the right decisions. In this type of situation, knowing our true costs in time and resources will allow us to respond to sudden change in a more intelligent manner. Even if you think you'll never encounter overwhelming changes, the information you learn from asking yourself this question will aid you in staying ahead of the daily changes you do encounter.

Just as the first question helps us get ahead of change, the second question prepares us to deal with change. The key is to answer the questions simultaneously. The most efficient time to learn the true cost of time and money for a task is when we're analyzing the task, breaking it apart. Keeping the answers to questions one and two separate is critical; but remember, as you make adjustments based on your answers to the first question, you may very well need to alter the answer to the second question.

Third, *what questions are new employees asking, and what can we learn from them?* Nobody has a fresher perspective on a department or company than the person who has just been hired or has just transferred in from a different location or department. Yet, our natural tendency is to indoctrinate them quickly into the culture and process of what needs to be done — so quickly, in fact, that we give up the rich input they can offer us as outsiders. Anyone who has children knows how many questions a toddler can ask and how many times they ask them at just the wrong time. But when we really take the time to stop and think about what they are asking, we find ourselves wondering why we didn't ask the same question.

New employees are the same way. They see things with an innocent eye, and they are not jaded in their thinking by the existing culture or processes of the company. Rather, new employees, by the virtue of being new, have a totally different perspective of the workplace. If we are to deal with change, we need to harness the resources of new employees, and, for that matter, anyone else who can bring a different perspective to our workplace. Only new people or those truly from the *outside* will have the capability to look objectively at our workplace and to challenge the things we do and the way we do them. True, they don't understand the workplace as well as the people who have been doing the work, but that's the whole point — they don't understand the workplace — and they don't understand the culture that can pervade the workplace to a point where we operate the same way much longer than we should. Naturally, when we operate the same way for too long, we become much less flexible in adapting to change until it's too late. The roots of chaotic change are not sown by what occurs suddenly, but from what is not sown daily: being aware of our environment and why we do what we do.

Within any organization, it's important to establish a process that allows the questions, thoughts, and perspectives of new employees to be heard and understood. We need to understand what they are saying — not just the content of the question or the idea, but the driving force behind the question or idea. When we understand the reasons for the questions, then we are able to determine the underlying meaning or concerns. By taking the time to listen to new employees, we open ourselves to being more aware of change and more adaptable as we respond to change.

When using new employees as a sounding board for change, realize that they will not always readily respond to management. This attitude is natural because they believe management controls whether they have a job or not. The key to getting around this barrier is to use other employees, peers, or mentors to provide them with an ear they can trust. The mentors and peers must maintain close relationships to determine what is being said and why it is being said. By using existing employees in this type of role, you also receive input from experienced people who can help to identify change as it occurs on a daily basis. If other employees are not available due to the size of a business, then other means need to be established. These may include informal, relaxed meetings that are non-threatening in nature, or feedback mechanisms, ranging from comment cards to self-evaluation tools. How a feedback process is set up will determine the quality of the information received, but it is more important that we do something to tap into the wealth of information new people can provide as we attempt to identify and deal with change.

The final question we need to ask ourselves when learning how to thrive in a period of change is personal in nature: *what would change if someone else came in to do my job?* Ex-CEO of General Electric, Jack Welch, first made this question famous, using it with his managers as a tool to determine what needed to be changed. The problem we have with this question is its personal nature. It is the type of question that begs us to find failure in what we do, and our human nature is not inclined to look for failure in ourselves. The whole idea simply runs counter to the fact that we all believe what we do is so essential to our employer that there is nothing we can do differently. The rub is in separating what we may personally believe is not important and what may be critically important to the business. Our nature is to focus on what we view as important. We must be cautious and proceed with care.

For example, when one person inherits another person's job, that new person may suddenly have piles of files thrust upon them that in many cases don't make any sense at all. When this occurs, there are two approaches to take. The first is to read through every file and attempt to emulate each activity or process represented. The other is to review only those few files that are deemed essential and place all of the others in an out-of-the-way location. Staying with this approach, the new employee can begin to do his or her job, accessing the piles of files stashed away only if needed. Finally, after a reasonable period of time has elapsed, the "other" files can be taken from the out-of-the-way location and thrown away. With this very simple approach, the new employee has reworked the process. The secret is to rework the process while you are still in the same position and still dealing with the same departments, the same customers, and the same daily challenges.

To successfully address the fourth question, we have to be able to gain a fresh perspective, which begins by continuously challenging our thinking based on the first three questions. Unless we are successfully asking ourselves the first three questions — and answering them — we cannot begin to ask ourselves what someone else would do if they came in to do our jobs. We can also gain insight on perspectives by finding out what others in similar positions are doing and, more important, what they are *not* doing. By developing a network with others and creating a comfort level, you can get beyond the results of projects and talk about the individual steps and processes used to complete the tasks at hand. We also gain insight by examining other industries and not just ones that are similar to ours.

Looking at what we do is, and always will be, the most difficult task. We find it much easier to see needed changes in others than to identify areas in our own job that need to be changed. Failure to examine what we do by asking ourselves this final question deprives us of valuable insight. We will have trouble seeing the change that occurs on a daily basis, and we will be so occupied dealing with change in our own job that our ability to thrive in the midst of chaos will be diminished.

The role of this question is very much like the instructions we receive from a flight attendant about using the oxygen mask. Flight attendants tell us to secure our own masks before helping those around us. Why? Unless we are receiving oxygen, we will not be able to assist others. When we challenge what we do and make the necessary adjustments, we'll be in a better position to deal with change when it occurs around us.

Change and our ability to thrive in the midst of change can be overwhelming, even for the best of people. The best approach to change is to not allow it to overwhelm us, asking these four questions on a regular basis:

1. What do we do as a business that drains resources from our company or department?

2. Do we know the true cost, in time and money, of each activity that we perform as a company or department?

3. What questions are new employees asking, and what can we learn from them?

4. What would change if someone else came in to do my job?

When thinking about these questions, keep the row of dominoes in mind. Remember the impact each domino has on the others when they are standing close to each other. Nothing we do is done in isolation; nothing we decide is an independent decision. Rather, everything we do impacts something, somewhere. Our ability to understand how and why these actions and decisions affect each other increases our ability to deal with change. Our goal is to avoid being blindsided by change, to learn to monitor it, to be conscious of it, and to place ourselves in a position to influence it. Viewing our activities as a string of dominoes allows us to be prepared — not just to experience change, but to thrive in its midst.

ABOUT
MARK HUNTER

*M*ark Hunter works with people and companies helping them present their messages more effectively. He offers consulting, seminars, and keynote speeches. Mark spends more than 100 days a year traveling, working with companies and individuals. From corporate board rooms to small town sales calls, Mark's communication strategies make a difference in people's lives. The foundation for his work is 25 years of management experience. He knows exactly what it takes to communicate effectively with many types of people in various situations. Beginning with managing a fast-food restaurant at the age of sixteen to spearheading the building of a 900-person sales team for a major corporation, Mark has held leadership positions in three multi-national corporations. Mark's extensive background in sales and marketing leadership enables his strategies to be on target with today's environment.

Contact information:
Mark Hunter
MJH & Associates
15633 Underwood
Omaha, NE 68118
Phone: (402) 445-2110
Fax: (402) 445-0942
E-mail: MarkJHunter@email.msn.com

THE RCA² FORMULA TO CHANGE

by Olita F. Williams

On a hot, humid morning in Birmingham I got up to go to work. I was only 14 years of age and this was my very first job and my very first day of work! I remember the excitement of getting dressed, making sure my hair was combed, putting on some of my sample Avon lipstick, Pink Mist, and sneaking into my sister's "Here's My Heart" perfume. I made sure that I had my purse with me. I kept going over in my mind all the polite things I was supposed to say, how I was to smile and, most importantly, how to accomplish what would be expected of me.

Up until now, my world had been consumed with dolls, books, and the stories Mama told me about her job as a maid. She would bring home magazines such as *McCalls, Redbook, Ladies Home Journal, Look,* and *House Beautiful* to show me what nice things people had in their homes, and she stressed how important it was for me to learn to be independent so that I could take care of myself and also have nice things.

I had been very persistent with Mama about working. Every other day I asked her when I could go to work. I needed my own money so that I could go on the beach trip to Florida with the other neighborhood children. Finally, one afternoon when Mama came in very tired and was making dinner she said, "Honeybunch, I think I got somebody you can go work for next week, but I don't think you're ready." I replied, "Ooh, Mama, I can't wait!"

As my big day arrived, I stood in the front door waiting for Mrs. Woods' arrival. My heart was beating fast because it was my day to prove to Mama and the world that I was ready to work. I had been waiting so long for this. Mama told me, "If you do a good job, maybe you can get more work."

When Mrs. Woods arrived, I climbed into the back seat of her car, like all maids. As we walked into her home she introduced me to her cute little girl, who had the most beautiful, blonde, curly hair I had ever seen, and to the child's nanny. After giving me a brief tour of her house, she explained what chores I needed to do that day. She said, "My nanny will fix you a sandwich for lunch at noon, I will be back to pick you up around 4:30 today." I replied, "Yes, M'am."

As soon as she backed out of the driveway, I put my purse on the table and started with the kitchen chores. I had to defrost the refrigerator, which was not an easy task. I began by boiling hot water and putting it up in the freezer compartment so that it could melt down the ice. In order to wipe out the lower section of the refrigerator, I had to remove everything. Once that task was completed, I put some Arm & Hammer baking soda in it to absorb any odors and to give it a fresh, clean smell. As I surveyed my work, I was so proud because I knew I had done a good job!

I moved to the next item on my list, which was the stove. In those days, we had to paint on a very strong mixture to clean and cut the grease on the range. Although it was called "Easy Off," I still can't make the connection with what was so easy about it. Not only did it smell terrible, if it came in contact with your skin, it would burn. I put on my gloves and let that Easy Off sit for an hour or so, then used a damp cloth to wipe off the dark, foul smelling foam from inside the oven, as well as all of the top burners. Continuing with my list, I mopped and waxed the kitchen floor, cleaned all the counter tops, and washed out the trash container. Vacuuming the dining room, den and living room was a breeze. I sang as I dusted the candelabra, lamps, and each of the unique items found in these rooms. They were beautiful and reminded me of what I had seen on the pages of the Sears and JC Penney catalogs. All of the crystal pieces looked exactly as they did in the magazines. Mama had a few nice pieces but not a complete set. I had already decided that I wanted to have a complete set when I grew up.

Around noon, I ate my sandwich and drank the Kool-Aid that the nanny had prepared. I was exhausted, yet I still had to finish cleaning the bathroom, tackle the ironing, and sweep the front porch. I decided to sweep the front porch because I could go outside and see where I was. As I swept the porch and dusted the chairs, I noticed other maids in the neighborhood, sweeping and cleaning windows. I felt so grown up at that point, but it also made me realize that Mama did this every day. It was only early afternoon and I was already tired, hot, and weary, and a lot of chores remained on the list.

The challenge of ironing was now facing me. I quickly finished cleaning the bath and headed upstairs to the attic area to start ironing. There were three baskets of clothes! It was obvious that the clothes were starched because they were sprinkled down and rolled up so they would have some dampness for ironing. There was no steam iron in those days, only a sprinkler bottle with water to dampen the clothes more, and a hard pressing from me!

Ironing all of the flat items would be easy, so I started with the pillow cases, table napkins, and handkerchiefs. The heat was unbearable up in that area, and although I had a little fan blowing, I was sweating profusely due to the suffocating humidity. I realized that what was left were shirts, pleated skirts, and blouses, along with a few ruffled dresses for the little girl. As I stood there, I thought *this is too much to do for such a small amount of money. Maybe she wants me to come back to finish all of this work.* Looking at my watch, I thought about all that I had accomplished, but I knew I could not finish ironing all three baskets of clothes before Mrs. Woods got home. I had my very first big revelation that day as I learned about extremely hard work that resulted in only a little pay.

Even at an early age, I knew that most colored women worked as maids for as little as $5 to $8 per day. I did my math and realized that was less than one dollar per hour, depending on how long you stayed for the day. I thought about all of the hard work I had done, the refrigerator, the stove, the mopping and waxing, and the bathrooms. What hard work this was! I compared the dollar value to milk, eggs, and a loaf of bread. Then I thought about the cost of my trip to the beach, which was $12, and I realized I would need to do another day's work to have enough money.

I began to think about how things are not always easy or fair. I felt cheated and thought there must be another way to earn money. All of a sudden, I could hear Mama saying to me, "The movement is about having a better life."

Growing up in Birmingham, Alabama, as a colored girl certainly had its challenges. Yes, right there in the "Heart of Dixie" and in the center of the Civil Rights movement stood a city polluted by the smog from the steel mills and minds that were polluted because of all the chaos. The city received national attention for its inability to accept change.

As a little girl I often thought, "What's so hard about changing and letting everybody do what he/she wants to do?" My Sunday school teacher Mrs. Carter, who had a beautiful smile and wore flowered hats, told me "we are all God's children," so why all the fuss? Little did I know the magnitude of what was happening around me would change the nation.

As one of eight children and the daughter of a Baptist preacher, I felt safe in life. Daddy prayed hard, loud, and long every day over the food, so to me that took care of the heaven stuff, and Mama was at home to look after us each day, except when she went to work. I had no real reason to feel threatened. Daddy would discuss current events at the dinner table and tell us to be careful and mind our own business. Of course, we had very little business because we went to our own school, played in our own neighborhood, and to safeguard it all, he took us everywhere in his car. We did not ride the buses. Why in the world would anyone want to change what we had, or not like what we were doing? It seemed fine to me.

So if this movement thing was to give me a better life, I guess I needed to make some changes. I began thinking out loud, "If I could do well in school, make good grades and get a quality education, then I could have a better life!" It all started to make sense to me, and I was ready to focus my attention in another direction. I made the decision that day that I did not want to be a maid because it required hard work with little reward. I also felt a deeper appreciation for all that Mama had done. It was obvious that I had to change my life!

As I went downstairs in the Woods' house, I felt so much better, and it was so much cooler because I had taken a mental load off my shoulders! Looking for a cool spot to sit down near the window air conditioner, I walked into the den where the nanny was so I could sit and watch the "Edge of Night," the only soap opera I understood well enough to follow. The little girl was lying on the sofa, so I could not sit there; plus, she looked at me as if the area were off limits. I then found a spot in the living room on the beautiful white brocade sofa. I was exhausted and just wanted to rest. From where I was sitting I could peek around the corner at the tv without the nanny seeing me.

The next sound I heard was Mrs. Woods in her very proper, Southern voice asking me, "Olita dear, are you not feeling well?" I sat up quickly, wiped my mouth and replied, "Yes M'am." She had a very startled look on her face and even seemed very pale to me. I guess she could not imagine the fact that I had gone to sleep on the job, and to make matters worse, on her white brocade sofa. I could see the nanny peeking around the corner at me, and I wondered why she had not awakened me! When Mrs. Woods asked if I had finished all of my chores, I replied, "Everything except some of the ironing, but I can come and finish on another day." I asked if she was going to pay me, and she gave me a hard-earned $8 for the day.

As we left her house for the drive home, I was so excited, I felt so free, and I felt that I had done a good job even though it was not a complete job. Normally, maids rode in the back seat, but I was so free in my mind that I opened the door and got into the front seat of the car. At least I could feel the air conditioner better there. Our drive to my home was quick and quiet, but I had made a new discovery about myself and I felt great. What a revelation it was!

As we drove up to my home, Mama was on the front porch. Mrs.

Woods asked if I would have Nancy come out to the car to speak to her. We said our polite good byes, and I got out of the car. As I walked up the sidewalk, Mama came down with this little smile on her face but walked right past me to the car. I realized at that moment, that, although I may have disappointed her, somehow she was not upset. I knew everything would be all right. Mama had known all along that it was a learning experience I needed and she had let me get it.

When Mama came into the house, she said, "Mrs. Woods thought you did a good job on the housework, but she understood that you were a little young, and there were three baskets of clothes, so I'll be going up there later this week to complete the ironing for her." She said, "I knew you were not ready for this. You like books, reading, and drawing. Being a maid is hard work." I defended myself by telling her about all the work and the amount of clothes that needed to be ironed. She agreed and admitted that she did not know there was going to be that much ironing, but we both knew she had proved her point. I assured her that I understood and let her know how much I appreciated how hard she worked for us. She said, "That's why you need to change your mind and keep it on those books." I agreed to do so, and from that point on, I had a feeling of what change was all about. It didn't always feel good, but I could get through it. If I knew what I did not want, it could certainly help me focus on what I did want!

I did make the beach trip that year. I earned enough money from my sisters and from saving my allowance. I even had extra money to buy some more books that summer.

Change meant doing something different to me. It meant going in a different direction from others at times. As I began to understand change, the Civil Rights movement began to make more sense to me. As a little colored girl in the south, change was consistent. We saw it, we felt it, and we had to decide quickly how to manage it!

As I matured and continued to hear about the Civil Rights movement and the changes that needed to take place to make our country a better place, I began to feel and understand that change was here to stay, and it was not as easy as I had thought. Just doing what Mrs. Carter, my Sunday school teacher, had told us was not enough. I turned my focus to school and read more, studied harder, and concentrated on having a better life. Throughout my elementary and high school days I was an honor student and graduated from high school as a member of the Honor Society. It did not stop there; I went on to college after a marriage and divorce, studied for seven years at night, worked a forty hour week, and used student loans to get my undergraduate degree. I knew about change and being determined to make changes.

The Civil Rights movement gave all of us a sense of peace over a period of time. We accepted it, and many people from the pulpits, the White House, the classrooms, and the courtrooms all used that "change" to their own advantage.

I now see change as a part of our daily bread! Each day we bite, chew, or swallow some phase of a change. To enjoy our lives, careers, and prosperity, the change has to be within us. Accepting this at an early age had its advantages for me.

My experience while growing up gave me a sense that I would always be dealing with some changes in my life and with having to make decisions or choices for my own personal and professional growth. I learned to make a lot of positive choices, like not becoming a maid or just settling for the status quo. With time, each step became easier in my growth cycle because I learned to manage myself. I feel that is what the Civil Rights movement gave me, an opportunity to understand that change was okay and would be all right with time.

As a speaker, consultant, and coach, I am often asked by my audiences or clients how I got started with my career, or they want me to share some pointers on how to do what I am doing. I used to answer with words of encouragement. In the role of a coach, I would question the individual to make him/her aware of answers from within. After a while, I started to think about what I could say to be more effective because most of the questions were about making changes.

Finally one evening as I landed at Hartsfield International Airport in Atlanta, I realized that I had a big smile on my face. It was the Speaker-Facilitator high! All of the feedback had been positive, and I even had a return invitation to speak. Life was beautiful!

As I drove along interstate I-85, I pondered the questions I am often asked, such as "How did you get started? What can I do to get started now? They won't let me do anything on my job; what should I do?" I would usually say, "Just do it," or "Make up your mind." It was so easy to say "go for it!" Deep down inside I wanted to give people ideas to help spark their own creativity.

As I reflected back over my life, my career, and the many challenges I had faced, I recalled four common elements present at each event in my life experiences: *responsibility, commitment, accountability*, and a good *attitude* to square it all off. I knew I had discovered something. A light came on inside my head. This was the answer I could share with people and feel good about.

Being a former IBM employee who had lived in a world of acronyms for years, I knew that I needed some alphabet soup, so I coined the **RCA^2 Formula**. This formula has many uses.

In today's workplace and in our personal lives, we are faced with many changes accompanied by many challenges. We live in a global environment where it is no longer important how only Americans work and play. Our lives and work are becoming part of a worldwide concept, which needs to be accepted by each of us. The 21st century demands that we be adaptable! The RCA^2 Formula can be helpful to us as we establish ourselves in this new global environment! Let's examine the formula to understand how it can help us cope with the challenges of change.

R
RESPONSIBILITY

Responsibility is the state, quality, or fact of being responsible.

As responsible adults we take care of our required needs on a continuous basis. We pay our bills, file taxes, work at our jobs, and respond to our civic and social responsibilities. However, when it comes to our own personal goals and life purpose, we may falter. Often we shirk responsibility for this very important part of our lives.

When I coach clients about their careers or life situations, too often I hear the victim mentality. Some of the common statements are, "The company decided to move my position to another location," or "I know I need to do something, but I don't know what to do," and last but not least, "They won't let me have the next level, and I am the most qualified." If any of these statements sounds familiar, or somewhat similar, keep reading.

To be responsible means to become aware of the multitude of choices we have in any given situation. The choices we make on a daily basis reflect the way we feel about ourselves and different situations. Being responsible also means figuring out what we want in life and then acting on it. Paradoxically, finding out what we don't like is as valuable as finding out what we do like. No one knows better than you what is best for you. Therefore, your first priority in making a change is to become responsible for yourself. You can do this by creating what I call "My Want List," or you may want to develop a "If I Could, I Would List." You can use whatever method is necessary to help you make choices, but you cannot move forward until you know what it is you want to do.

Secondly, to support your choices when you have become a responsible person for your life, you must make yourself aware of the "payoffs" that are holding you where you are. Keep in mind that the "payoff" is whatever keeps you perpetually doing what you don't want to do. The fact that you have invested time in a situation does not give you the right to remain unchanged.

Thirdly, you must accept that with each challenge in life, something within forces you to handle it. As you do so, your self-esteem is raised considerably. Once you learn to trust that you will survive no matter what happens, you will experience change better, and whatever fears you may have had will disappear.

I experienced making choices for change early in life! I took on the responsibility needed to support my choices and eventually life became easier.

> *"The trick in life is not to worry about making wrong*
> *decisions, it is learning when to correct them!"*
>
> — Unknown Author

C
COMMITMENT

Commitment is the act of committing; a giving in charge or entrusting; to pledge to do something.

Once you have decided to become responsible for your life's purpose, you must take action by putting a plan in place to support the outcomes of your desires. In this area, many of us fall out of the lineup.

Over the years I have observed some of the reasons we fall out of the lineup. All of us have our own little "chatterbox" (talking brain), that appears whenever it realizes we want to focus on something. The chatterbox will tell you about all of the other things you could be doing, and it will tell you reasons why your new idea will not work. It may even pull you back to your old comfort zone, if you allow it. To fight off the chatterbox, you will need to learn to talk to it, and remind it that you are in control now and you are making a change. This is not an easy step because the chatterbox has invested time in keeping you where you are, and it wants to win.

Next you will need to establish or get involved with people who can support you. Learn to be around people who are open and supportive toward your ideas for growth. Why do you think we have "AA" and other support groups? They are there to help people make changes in their lives, if they commit to them. A commitment is established for the purpose of helping you move forward and stay focused on your desired outcome. To get the best results, you must give 100 percent! Know that the commitment is a part of your being responsible.

Perseverance and patience are extremely important to your commitment. You must be able to persevere, even when the chatterbox presents other circumstances. Persevere in your commitment and give it the time needed to materialize.

Patience must be exhibited deliberately; you must look at all areas of your life and determine how you can make the necessary adjustments to allow you to remain patient in a deliberate plan of action.

> *"I skate to where the puck is going to be,*
> *not to where it has been."*
>
> — Wayne Gretsky

A
ACCOUNTABILITY

Accountability is being answerable; capable of being explained.

Being accountable and answerable for your actions mean not blaming others. To be accountable means taking control of your life and moving to a position of power. This position of power creates the self-esteem and energy needed to pursue your desires. Learn to monitor where you are with your actions. This process will allow you to have more control of your expected outcomes and to adjust your plans when necessary.

Most importantly, be honest with yourself about your lack of progress when you are not taking the appropriate actions. No one has control over you but you. Your accountability to self is very important.

> *"I will be accountable for how my life is going. If I don't like how*
> *it feels, it is up to me to monitor my thoughts and change them."*
>
> — Unknown Author

A²
ATTITUDE

Attitude is a state of mind or feeling with regard to some situation or event.

This is the glue for the RCA² Formula. It enables all of the other elements to materialize effectively for you. Attitude is the way you approach a situation; it reflects your overall thoughts and feelings about a situation.

It is not enough to just have a positive attitude; you must display it! Your energy concerning any situation radiates into your environment. Attitude has a marked effect on everything you do and on how successful you are.

Maintain a positive and energized attitude about your purpose because it is the glue to make it all flow together.

"The first step in changing ourselves, if that is what we want to do, is to change our ATTITUDE about what we see outside of ourselves!"
— Unknown Author

As individuals or groups, we do not change just because we are asked to. We change when we find a way to be a part of the change and when our behaviors become a part of the process of change. It is only in that state of mind that a feeling of power emerges. Once we understand change and how we can use our own personal power to implement change, we begin to thrive!

ABOUT
OLITA F. WILLIAMS

O lita Williams is President of ATILO Training & Consulting Services, a practice that works with organizations to develop people performance that connects to the business strategy. She works with individuals to help them recognize their fullest potential and obtain it! As an accomplished seminar leader, keynoter, and consultant, Olita is known for her high energy and colorful presentation style that engages audiences and gets her invited back. Her 15 years of experience across several industries provides her with practical, hands-on experience in managing projects, facilitating meetings, providing career coaching, and delivering wide-ranging training programs. Olita's areas of expertise are customer service, sales, leadership development, resume writing, and interviewing skills. Some of her clients are Waste Management, IBM, Delta Airlines, AT&T, Drake Beam Morin, and Motorola. To stay current, Olita is active in the American Society of Training and Development and the National Speakers Association. She currently resides in Atlanta, Georgia.

Contact information:
Olita F. Williams
ATILO Training & Consulting Services
2647 Glenrose Hill
Atlanta, GA 30341-5785
Phone: (770) 938-4006
Fax: (770) 723-1498
E-mail: Atilofw@attglobal.net

RESISTANCE AND ORGANIZATIONAL CULTURE — A LEADER'S GUIDE TO CHANGE

by Mike Monahan

"*It must be considered that there is nothing more difficult to carry out, nor more doubtful of success, nor more dangerous to handle, than to initiate a new order of things. For the reformer has enemies in all those who profit by the old order, and only lukewarm defenders in all those who would profit by the new order, this lukewarmness arising partly from fear of their adversaries, who have the laws in their favor; and partly from the incredulity of mankind, who do not truly believe in anything new until they have had actual experience of it. Thus it arises that on every opportunity for attacking the reformer, his opponents do so with the zeal of partisans, the others only defend him halfheartedly, so that between them he runs great danger.*"

MACHIAVELLI — from *The Prince*

For those of us involved in helping organizations change, Machiavelli understated the challenge. Changing an organization, workgroup, or team is an onerous undertaking. When dealing with a group, one has entities equal to the number of members plus one — the group itself with whom you must interact. Much has been written about the resistance of individuals to change but less about the resistance of the group as an entity of its own. If one is responsible for the implementation of change in a group, you must be able to recognize how that group is likely to take to or resist the intended change. In this chapter, we will look at the assessment of group change readiness and some actions for producing the very best results in a changing group.

First, let's review the concept of resistance.

Basic Concepts in Resistance

Resistance is any opposition to a shift in the status quo. (Conner, 1992) It occurs because people are control-oriented. When expectations are disrupted, their ability to control their lives is minimized, and resistance is the result.

Expectations are disrupted most often when people perceive more danger, less opportunity, or a greater amount of ambiguity in a situation than they anticipated.

Resistance is a natural and inevitable reaction to loss of control. Its occurrence doesn't mean that something is wrong; it indicates that people are no longer able to operate as they expected to, and they are uncomfortable.

Both positively and negatively perceived changes lead to disruption, so people will not resist only changes that they see as negative. When people resist change, they are resisting the loss of control caused by their expectations being disrupted. As disruption increases, so does resistance. Therefore, strong resistance will always be the companion of major (significantly disruptive) change, whether or not people say they "like" it.

Individuals resist change when, from their frame of reference, the change appears to go against their values, makes them or others they care about emotionally upset, the knowledge base that they believe in rejects it, or it would require a shift in one or more of their well-established behavioral patterns.

Resistance to Negatively Perceived Change

When individuals see a change as negative (undesirable), their resistance reactions go through a predictable cycle. The model is based on Elizabeth Kubler Ross's work on responses to personal loss (Ross, 1969):

1. *Immobilization* is the initial reaction to a negatively perceived change (shock).

2. *Denial* is characterized by an inability to absorb new information into the current frame of reference.

3. *Anger* involves frustration with the change and often includes irrational and indiscriminate lashing out.

4. Afterward, people resort to *bargaining* to avoid the negative impact of change.

5. *Depression* is a normal response to major, negatively perceived change. The full extent of clinical depression, helplessness and hopelessness, is not usually found in organizational settings, but resignation to failure, a feeling of being victimized, a lack of emotional and physical energy, and disengagement from one's work are likely symptoms.

6. *Testing* helps people to regain a sense of control and to free themselves from feelings of victimization and depression

7. *Acceptance* involves realistically facing the change, but this is not necessarily synonymous with liking what has happened.

Resistance to Positively Perceived Change

Individuals also go through predictable reactions to changes they perceive as positive (desirable). Resistance is at its greatest during the Informed Pessimism stage, when individuals may respond by "checking out" publicly or privately. (Conner, 1992 & 2001)

1. Uninformed optimism is characterized by naïve enthusiasm based on insufficient data.

2. As major change unfolds, much of what we were promised does not come to pass, and much of what begins to take place we are unprepared for. This is called informed pessimism. If this pessimism should surpass a person's tolerance for doubt, the withdrawal from a change that occurs is called checking out (either privately — quit and stay — or publicly — quit and leave).

3. When the concerns of the informed pessimism begin to lessen, people move into hopeful realism (i.e., having a realistic understanding of the change and a sense of hope of moving through the transition successfully).

4. As more and more issues are resolved, people become increasingly confident. They then move into informed optimism.

5. They then can either complete the change or begin the cycle again via another change.

Resistance and Commitment

Both individuals and teams go through a process of committing to change. Commitment involves both thought and feeling reactions and may proceed at different rates. An important point to remember with regard to resistance is that people don't really resist change until they understand it. They may display confusion, but they are not at the point where they can be truly said to be resisting until they have a framework for how that change will affect them. (Conner, 1993 & 2001)

Commitment to a specific outcome is evident when people:

- Invest the necessary resources.
- Consistently pursue the goal.
- Reject ideas or action plans that are inconsistent with ultimate goal achievement.
- Stand fast in the face of adversity.
- Apply creativity, ingenuity, and resourcefulness.

GROUP RESISTANCE

Groups resist change through commitment to their current culture. Culture acts like a large rubber band, allowing individuals to make some progress towards change, but pulling everyone back close to the original point after the pressure diminishes. When managing change in a group or organization, it is necessary to not only be aware of individual resistance to change, but also of the attributes of the organizational or group culture that will support or resist change.

Anyone wanting to help an organization manage a change initiative must be aware of both individual and organizational attributes supportive or resistant to change. In preparing the way for success in change, a process of assessment should be completed that includes the following:

- *Determining the Compelling Reason to Change* — What is the reason for change stated in the most basic of terms for the organization and individuals? Leaders, or those inciting change, must be able to articulate the reason for such change in a way that leaves no doubt that the change is necessary for survival of the organization and a continuation of benefits for members of the organization.

- *Resources and Will to Complete the Process* — Many change initiatives fail because the leaders lack the will to see the process through to the end. Change disrupts routines and may result in a temporary decline in both effectiveness and efficiency. Group leaders must be willing to commit time, resources and significant patience to completion of the process.

- *Leadership Competencies in Management Staff* — Leading people through change requires the best in leadership. The ability to create a positive vision of the future, help people through the periods of uncertainty, and keep the group focused on moving forward is a challenging necessity. This process is made even more difficult by the almost certain likelihood of emerging dysfunctional behaviors in staff during stressful times of change. Dr. David Wadner, noted author and clinical psychologist, describes the phenomenon of regressive dependency as a major impediment to successful change. People undergoing changes in their life have a tendency to become self-focused, entitled and less likely to be creative, task focused, and energetic. Leadership is the antidote to regressive dependency. This author uses a variety of tools to measure managerial competency. Interviews, observations, and self-designed competency taxonomies have been very useful. In data-intensive, big-system changes, this author has found the use of a reliable, validated competency measurement tool, such as the Listen360 produced by Strategic Programs Inc. of Denver, Colorado, to be invaluable.

The Organizational Cultural Assessment — An extremely valuable tool in helping groups through change is to assess the group culture to look for attributes that will contribute or inhibit permanent change. Completion of the cultural assessment creates a picture of the readiness of the organization for change and allows for planning and implementing a much more effective change plan. This author conducts interviews with key or, depending on size, all group members and asks questions related to the following areas:

• *Rules/Policies*—The goal is to determine what the real or perceived rules and policies are that might hinder adoption of new processes or ways of doing business. Questions to ask may include: What rules and policies govern your work and activities? What policies might have to be changed before you can do things differently? In working with health care organizations, for example, there is always some regulatory or accrediting body that is blamed for the organization's faulty processes. People will say, "We have to do that, JCAHO requires it . . . or it is a Medicare requirement." Compliance with Medicare regulations or meeting Joint Commission for the Accreditation of Healthcare Organization's standards is important, but those requirements are not usually impediments to enhanced performance or organizational change. On the other hand, union work rules, overtime policies, and human resource policies may have a legitimate impact and will require some action before changes can be made.

• *Goals/Measure* — It is critical to determine what gets measured and how goals are set in an organization to be changed. Questions to ask would include: How would the proposed changes affect current measurement standards? How are goals set around here? How do you know when you have met or exceeded standards? Do you regularly meet your goals? This author is currently working with an organization that needs to improve productivity and wants to implement a system that requires a strong focus on individual accountability for work performance. Up until now, the organization functioned by setting team goals and measuring team activities, not individual accomplishment. The proposed changes may be good for the organization but are different from the current method of operation and are likely to result in cultural push-back.

• *Customs/Norms* — It is critical to understand how work gets done in a team, workgroup, or organization by determining factors such as pace, sense or urgency, "go to" people, level of courtesy, conflict, and relationships with other groups. Questions to ask would include: How do things get done around here? What kind of organization is this? Who gets things done? What gets in the way of getting things done? How do you relate to other departments, teams, etc? A very illustrative question is: What one word best describes this team, group, or organization? In a recent change project, this author was told, "We let people pretty much decide what they are going to do each day." The response to the "one word" question was "loose." A change project intended to increase personal responsibility and productivity in this organization would be destined for difficult implementation.

• *Training* — Training and the level of skills in the workgroup are important determinants of successful change. One must find out if training is viewed as important and if the need is being met. Will there be training resources to support the new skills required? Questions to ask include: What is the level of training here? Do people get the training they need to do their jobs well now? Will training be available for supporting new processes? Does management support training? How? Answers to these questions will help change leaders determine the availability of resources and commitment of the leadership.

• *Ceremonies* — Ceremonies are symbols of what organizations hold to be important, and they often reflect traits of the "old way" people are reluctant to give up. Questions to ask include: What kinds of things do you celebrate around here? When was your last public ceremony? What was it about?

• *Management Behaviors* — Presence, degree of involvement, perceptions related to support for the change and past decision-making are examples of management behaviors that reflect possible positive or negative support for change. There are three important dimensions to be measured here. One is the actual ability of managers to influence staff based on the manager's skills and personality. Another is the manager's own support of or resistance to the changes. The third is staff beliefs about motivations, aims and the general trust level of managers, especially senior management removed from daily contact with individual staff. Questions to ask include: How does management support changes here? How do your leaders help you when you are undergoing stressful times? Do your leaders support change? How do you think your managers support this change? Will leadership provide you with the resources you need?

• *Rewards and Punishments* — All behavior in a workgroup or organization is rewarded: positively or negatively, directly or indirectly, and/or intentionally or unintentionally. It is important to review formal rewards systems to determine alignment with the intended changes. It is also critical to determine what behaviors get rewarded or punished informally. Questions include: What behaviors get rewarded around here? What sort of incentives are provided for exceptional behavior? What gets punished around here? What sorts of things do people do less of because something bad happens when they do them?

• *Communications* — How people talk to each other and how the workgroup or organization receives and sends information is critical knowledge in helping with change. Successful change initiatives depend on clear, complete, and extensive communications. Change leaders need to know if the communications style of the group will support or hinder change efforts. Questions to ask include: How do people communicate around here? How open is communication? What percentage of "the word" is missed by people? What gets in the way of good communications? What people or departments aid or impair good communications?

• *Physical Environment* — The physical environment has an impact not only on the psychology of the work environment but also may impact the ability to effect change. Ask questions such as: What about the physical environment will support or hinder the proposed changes? What about the physical environment gets in the way of getting things done? What do you like best about the physical environment?

• *Organizational Structure* — Quite often the organizational structure is the focus of the change effort, but it is always important to know how the organizational structure currently exists and functions. We need to know how hierarchical the organization is. Who owns what resources and decision-making authority? How many layers are there from top to bottom? Questions to ask include: How is this organization structured? Who reports to whom? Is your organizational chart accurate? How much decision-making authority does each level of managers/supervisors have?

• *Angels and Ogres* — In every workgroup or organization, there are individuals who make things happen and support the actions of those trying to make things better. There are also naysayers, obstructionists, and downright troublemakers who may make the change more difficult. These people may be members of the change target group or may be in a position of influence over the group. Ask questions such as: Whom will we have to convince to make this work? Who always stands in the way of getting things you need? Whom can we count on to help us in this process?

OVERCOMING CULTURAL RESISTANCE

Armed with the information from the cultural assessment, plan your change initiatives accordingly. The following is an eight-step process for helping plan a change initiative that takes into consideration the likelihood of resistance based on cultural traits.

• Build the case for change — What is your compelling reason to change? This reason should be defined in a way that is easily understood by all. Appeal to both emotion and reason. The group members should understand the need for the change and feel that the change will benefit them in some way. At the very least, they must realize that failure to change will have personal consequences.

- Define a roadmap for the change — The group will benefit from less uncertainty. Bridges describes the space between the "Now" and the "Future" as the "Neutral Zone." He goes on to state that fear of the neutral zone is the single greatest impediment to making changes. (Bridges, 1991) A roadmap helps the team see the way past the neutral zone.
- Develop a communications and involvement strategy — Don't assume groups will automatically figure out ways to get the information they need. Often, the more they need information, the more they distort the message or don't listen. Plan for redundancies in style and amount of information provided. Get as many people as possible involved in the change process; that helps both enhance communications and reduce resistance.
- Design/redesign the organization to support the changes — An organization requires structural or operational redesign that will support the desired changes. Information systems, communications technology, reporting functions, physical location, and staff competencies must meet the needs of the changed processes.
- Plan for implementation — Shoddy, haphazard implementation will guarantee poor acceptance of the change and a decreased likelihood of sustainability. A detailed plan including all of the steps listed in this article is needed. The plan should include Bridge's steps of 1. Ending the old way, 2. Transitioning the neutral zone, and 3. Celebrating new beginnings. (Bridges, 1991) Plans should include start and stop dates, resources, measures of success, and details about who is responsible for what.
- Implement the change — Again, roll out the changes using the Bridge's Transition Model. Keep people informed and deal with resistance proactively. Be prepared to make modifications to your plan as needed, but don't just give in to resistance.
- Monitor and evaluate progress — Using the measurement indicators specified in the plan, keep close tabs on progress.
- Renew the organization — Noer calls this "Healing the Organization." (Noer, 1996) People suffer during the change process.

They lose face, have issues with competency, deal with confusion, and experience real pain and loss. Change leaders need to have an equal emphasis on results and human needs. Give people an opportunity to talk, express their feelings, and learn new ways. Establish rewards for success but encourage those who are at least trying.

BUILDING A CHANGE READY ORGANIZATION — THE "R2R" FACTOR

Concluding this chapter is a review of some leverage skills to help build and maintain teams and organizations that are more likely to adapt to changes in the future. The actions of leaders are the single most important determinant in predicting team change success. As change, and resistance to change, will be a factor in every organization over time, the effective leader will build "Resistance to resistance" in the team as a function of everyday activity. Building this "R2R Factor" is a process that involves the following:

1. Building a high "R2R" culture.

2. Recognizing and supporting members of the group who are early adaptors and capable of supporting change.

3. Providing leadership to overcome resistance.

Building a High "R2R" Culture

Use the Cultural Assessment Model presented earlier in this chapter to pinpoint those areas of the organization you need to focus on in enhancing "R2R." Intentionally develop, manage, and control the following:

Rules/Policies — Make certain you develop and regularly review rules and policies to determine their applicability, enforceability, and necessity.

Goals/Measure — Make certain the goals of the team or organization are clear, agreed-upon, and achievable. Pay attention to how you measure success and make it clear how the actions of each individual are tied to results.

Customs/Norms — Build team values consistent with the needs of your organization. Monitor the emerging informal norms and challenge publicly those that are inconsistent with the needs and values of the organization.

Training — Provide necessary training to ensure competency in the technical aspects of the job. Also pay attention to learning needs in human performance areas such as team member behaviors, leadership, negotiation, and change adaptation. Also make certain the training messages, both intended and coincidental, are consistent with the values you are trying to support.

Ceremonies — Look at the things you celebrate publicly in your organization. Humans are intensely responsive to symbolic gestures. Your ceremonies have a big impact on your staff's beliefs about the importance of behaviors so recognized.

Management Behaviors — In his article, "The Manager's Job: Folklore and Fact," Henry Mintzberg suggests that managers are often responsible for a range of activities very different from those described in textbooks or presumed important by the individual. (Mintzberg, 1990) In fact, leaders of teams and organizations are symbols of the well-being of the organization, responsible for community wellness, and drivers of the organizational culture.

Rewards and Punishments — Watch what behaviors are rewarded and punished. As self-evident as it appears, generally, behaviors that are rewarded are repeated and behaviors that are punished are extinguished. Informal rewards and punishments are often insidious and just as powerful as formal rewards and punishments.

Communications — People talk to each other, but they don't necessarily communicate on a level necessary to promote a culture that can adapt to change. Build communications channels by promoting dialogue between individuals, departments, functional areas, or any other divisions of your people. Support the notion that it is better to air issues than suppress them. Reward open discussions through your actions and words.

Physical Environment — Make the most of the physical environment. Assemble people according to workflow enhancement. Don't build barriers to communicating and appropriate socializing. Pay attention to physical dimensions such as heat, air conditioning, cleanliness, and safety.

Organizational Structure — Don't be bound by past experiences in designing the structure of your organization. Reporting requirements, levels of supervision, divisions of labor, and staff functions should support the purpose of the organization. Be aware of the need for future change and ask yourself if the organizational structure is adaptable.

Ogres and Angels — Evaluate the members of your team or organization. Determine who produces great results. Determine who is an early adapter. Support and develop them! Find the rabble-rousers who disrupt the flow of work and create conflict. Make them change their ways or get rid of them!

Recognizing Early Adaptors

Early adapters aren't all young, aggressive people, on the fast track to high-tech success. Age, income, and ambition are not deciding factors in becoming an early adapter. Instead, it is a composite of attitude, perspective, and values. Change relies on agility, the feature that separates those who can quickly detect and respond to changing events from those who are overwhelmed by them. The following characteristics, first described by Robert Gilbreath (Gilbreath, 1986), are typical of early adapters:

• Change Consciousness — Change is the constant for today and tomorrow. Early adapters look for signposts of change everywhere, constantly on the alert for trends and differences, whether they appear in technology, politics, fashion, lifestyles, or culture. They absorb information without regard to its immediate relevance. Then, the information is assessed and its usefulness determined.

• Extreme Sensitivity To External Forces — Early adapters look to stakeholders, customers and society to determine emerging needs, indicators of satisfaction/dissatisfaction, and changing circumstances that will require different organizational behaviors.

• Realistic View of Today — Early adapters aren't prisoners of yesterday's choices. They know surviving a future of change means shedding the burden of fixed assets — to start lean, and keep their options open as long as possible. Agility is the key. Early adapters choose adaptive skills and flexible technology so that they never become, in Thoreau's words, "tools of their tools."

• Craving For Alternatives — Organizations seeking change should be wary of process zealots, who insist that their one way is the only way. Members who are committed to improvement build an ability to adapt in all circumstances.

• Goal-driven — Early adapters embrace results rather than methods, choosing to accomplish rather than just comply. This is not to say they break rules simply for the sake of being different. They simply see rules as tools justified only by their effectiveness, and are not afraid to bend them, change them, or throw them out when they no longer work.

• An Appreciation of the Power of Synergy — This means a bringing together of parts to create a greater whole. (Covey, 1989) Mastering change requires an ability to combine disparate efforts and methods of different groups. Early adapters who excel in this capability not only bring value to the organization personally, they also build this in their fellow team members.

• Future Vision — Although it can be sudden, change seldom attacks without warning. Early adapters peek into the future, over the horizon of their immediate needs, in order to sense impending change and better prepare for it. They also have excellent peripheral vision, seeing not only their goals, but also conditions and environments surrounding them. To hone this skill, early adapters develop broad interests and far-reaching concerns.

• Broad Experience — Early adapters are eclectic in their careers, constantly in motion and seldom in a rut. They abhor doing the same thing over and over again. Nonlinear success demonstrates adaptability and sustained confidence—attractive features for anyone facing change.

• Flexible Perspective — Early adapters can rise up for the big picture or zoom in for a close-up. They can relate to nitty-gritty production problems as well as high-level strategic issues, and are often seen translating for others — helping them make intuitive leaps from the big picture to the small component — and vice versa.

• Knowing When To Let Go — Early adapters know when to continue with what works, but more important, they know when to admit defeat, let go, and move on. They take the long view, and are decidedly expedient, pragmatic and reasonable.

• Love of Proximity — Early adapters are participants, not spectators. They demand the right to determine their own actions and manage their own careers, and won't settle for routine, arms-length relationships with their work. They want to be proximate — to be intensely involved and an integral part of what they're doing.

Supporting Early Adapters

You may agree that change is a desirable goal, but you may not appreciate how perishable true early adapters can be. They are demanding and dynamic, and the very features that make them such a valuable asset make their support a continuous challenge. If you're going to manage change, you must also manage your early adapters. (Gilbreath, 1986)

• Don't Stand In Their Way — Traditional organizational loyalty is perceived differently by early adapters. Early adapters are looking for congruence with their own career, ideals, and potential. Early adapters want to make a contribution. Their power and energy will not be restrained, and smart managers wouldn't want it any other way.

• Earn Their Allegiance — They take no respect for granted, nor do they expect it automatically for themselves. Once "buy-in" was expected of all employees, but today it must be earned. That is why it is virtually impossible for regressive or reactionary managers to command or even coexist with early adapters.

• Give Them A Light Leash — Pragmatism, innovation, and resourcefulness characterize early adapters. They need a wide berth and plenty of discretionary authority to energize these traits. They are not just followers, but pioneers, who abhor prescriptive procedures and "rule by rote."

• Display Your Values — Early adapters know that unless they share your values, a confrontation is inevitable. Just as they love proximity to work in terms of time and space, they demand a certain degree of "value proximity." In the long run, this leads to mutual trust—a vital ingredient in any relationship with early adapters.

Early adapters tend to surface when conditions are ripe for change. Early adapters ride the waves of change. They know the risks and have the skills. You should know them!

"R2R" Leadership Tools

Tool #1 — Build an effective work force:

Hire good people — This sounds simple and yet most managers find it incredibly difficult. Look specifically for the following traits in new hire candidates:

• A strong performance ethic

• A cooperative, not a competitive, mindset

• A high level of communication skills

• An expressed desire to get along with others

• Appreciation of complementary skills of fellow staff members

Tool #2 — Create a positive work environment:

Make feedback, recognition, and reward part of your regular staff meeting agenda — Remember: recognized and rewarded results are repeated! Become mutually accountable for results — Make yourself answer to your staff for your role and responsibilities. A simple tool to do this is to ask your staff daily:

• "What worked well today?"

• "What made you feel good about working here today?"

• "What are you proud of today?"

• "Who deserves special recognition today?"

• "What didn't work today?"

• "What caused problems today?"

- "What made you angry today?"
- "What took too long, or was too complicated?"
- "Are there any things that we did that took too many people or took too many actions?"
- "What did we have to do that didn't contribute to our purpose?"
- "What sorts of extraneous things did we attempt to do today?"

Tool #3 — Get results:

Develop and implement a measurement system in which every member of the team understands what is expected of them and how they will find out how well they are doing compared to these expectations. This system will need to include:

- A statement of the team's anticipated results with measures and performance standards for each result
- Statements of each individual's anticipated results with measures and performance standards for each of these results
- A clear picture of the priorities and relative importance of the team and individual results

Tool #4 — Be a leader:

- Be competent and decisive.
- Balance your demands for your staff's productivity with respect for your staff's production capability.
- Don't motivate others to oppose you.
- Expect the best and encourage your staff.
- Understand people as both individuals and groups.
- Create an environment in which failure is not fatal.
- Model successful behavior.

YOU CAN MAKE A DIFFERENCE

The success of your organization is directly related to the ability of your group to recognize the need for change, make the changes with a minimum of human and operational cost, and sustain the change. You can make a difference.

"There's always going to be a place in the world for one who will say, "I'll take care of it.'"

— Anonymous

References:

Bridges, W. (1991). *Managing Transitions: Making the Most of Change*. Reading, MA: Addison-Wesley.

Conner, D. (1992). *Managing at the Speed of Change*. New York: Random House.

Conner, D. (2001). *Leading at the Edge of Chaos: How to Create the Nimble Organization*. New York: Random House.

Covey, S. (1989). *The Seven Habits of Highly Effective People*. New York: Simon and Schuster.

Gilbreath, R. (1986). *Escape From Management Hell: Twelve Tales of Horror, Humor and Heroism*. San Francisco: Barrett-Kohler.

Gubman, E. (1998). *The Talent Solution: Aligning Strategy and People to Achieve Extraordinary Results*. New York: McGraw Hill.

Department of Health and Human Services Website (1998)

Kanter, R.M. (1983). *The Change Masters*. New York: Simon and Schuster.

Lewin, K. (1951). *Field Theory in Social Science*. D. Cartwright (Ed). New York: Harper & Row.

Lowery, J. Ed. (1997). *Culture Shift*. Chicago: AHA Press.

Mintzberg, H. (1990). "The Manager's Job: Folklore and Fact": *Harvard Business Review*. March-April 1990.

Monahan, M., Edited by: Smart, D. (1998). *Irresistible Leadership*. Roswell, GA: James and Brookfield Publishers.

Monahan, M., Edited by: Smart, D. (1998). *Where There's Change There's Opportunity*. Roswell, GA: James and Brookfield Publishers.

Noer, D. (1996). *Breaking Free: A Prescription for Personal and Organization Change*. San Francisco: Jossey-Bass.

Ross, E, (1969). *On Death and Dying*. New York: MacMillan Publishing

Wadner, D. (2001) Personal Conversations with Author.

ABOUT
MIKE MONAHAN

Mike Monahan is the managing partner for M2HRA, a human performance improvement consulting and training practice. Mike has worked as a manager and executive in several organizational settings. He has developed a particular interest in the needs of transforming organizations, focusing on helping teams and individuals improve performance, and tend to the human side of change. Mike conducts leader and manager competency development sessions and has a series of customizable training interventions for all levels of supervisors and managers. Mike is the co-author of the acclaimed books, Where There's Change There's Opportunity *and* Irresistible Leadership. *Mike has published numerous articles in professional journals. He is a frequent speaker at national conferences and has consulting clients ranging from small business practices to Fortune 500 companies. Mike's undergraduate degree is with honors from the University of Colorado as is his Masters Degree in Educational Administration and Supervision from Roosevelt University in Chicago.*

Contact information:
Mike Monahan
M2HRA
1153 Bergen Parkway, Suite M-181
Evergreen, CO 80439
Phone and Fax: (303) 674-3186
Voice Mail: (800) 759-2881
E-mail: M2HRA@aol.com

DISCOVERING HIDDEN OPPORTUNITIES IN CHANGE

by Dondi Scumaci

What comes immediately to mind when you hear the word *"change"*? In experiential workshops, I've watched thousands of people react spontaneously to simulated change. Even in these mock situations, people find change incredibly uncomfortable. Their first perception is often a sense of loss. Change means giving something up — losing something.

In reality, the "something lost" may be quite tangible — my job, my health, or the balance in my checking account. Even then, the something lost threatens the abstracts in my life — my security, my pride, or my independence.

In a workshop on the West coast, I met two women living the lessons of change in very different ways. They were both health care professionals, working for a large organization undergoing massive reorganization. These women and hundreds of their colleagues faced eminent lay offs, reassignments, and deep pay cuts.

The first woman talked with excitement about choosing a new career. Naturally, she was apprehensive about losing her job. At the same time she realized this situation was forcing her to step out of her comfort zone, learn new skills, and reevaluate her life goals. She said, "If I lose my job, I'm going to get out there and find the job of my dreams! I'm not sure what will happen, but one way or another this is going to turn out great."

Her colleague, on the other hand, was very bitter. She was angry at the organization for placing her in this position after years of faithful service. Clearly, she felt betrayed and abused.

Throughout the day, I couldn't help but notice the sharp contrast between these two people who were experiencing the same circumstances. One was taking notes furiously and participating completely. The other sat with her arms folded, rolling her eyes, and frequently checking her watch.

Several months later, I received an email from the first woman. She had not only survived the reorganization — she had received a huge promotion! I wrote back to congratulate her and could not resist asking, "How is your friend?" She gracefully replied, "Unfortunately, she was in the first round of layoffs."

Here's the real tragedy — that woman left the organization thinking something had been done to her, something had been taken from her. In reality, she was a volunteer casualty — a victim of her own response. Change knocked at the door of both women — only one of them recognized possibility and welcomed it in.

We do not always choose the events that touch our lives. We most certainly choose how we respond. In the end, our responses determine the quality of the journey and the destination.

It's easy to miss opportunity because change is a master of disguise. It may come as a wildfire, sweeping through the canyons of your life — threatening to consume what you have so carefully built. It may come as a thief in the night. You awaken to find that change has been there while you slept. Or, change may arrive as a box on your doorstep. Your first reaction may be, "I did not order this! Take it back!" In every case, change is a journey and a paradox. It is in the journey through change that we develop the strength to travel on.

You may be familiar with the four progressive stages of change — denial, resistance, exploration, and commitment. Recognizing the four stages of change may help us cope with change, but this book isn't about coping with change or even managing it. I don't want to just rise to the occasion. I want to use the occasion as a ladder in my life. I want to stand on the shoulders of change and pull myself up to a higher place!

Do you want to thrive in the midst of change? If you want to find possibility and discover the opportunity in change, translate the four stages into four milestones and travel with the principles of change. The milestones are your road map. The principles are your guides.

As we embark, think about a change you are currently navigating, or one that you have recently come through. Apply the goals and principles to your particular situation. Along the way you will find opportunities to access your "change-ability," challenge your assumptions, and measure your progress.

When first confronted by change or the sense that something is about to change, we are propelled into stage one — denial. Denial has its own language. Sometimes it sounds like fear. It screams out in self-preservation. Sometimes denial takes on a skeptical, cynical tone. Denial says:

"That will never happen."

"This won't last."

"That can't be true."

Denial pushes away even the most exciting, positive changes. Have you ever said, "This is too good to be true?" That is denial whispering in your ear, telling you that you aren't worthy of this goodness and that it won't remain with you long.

Listen closely for denial. The words used to express first reactions are important clues. They tell you a secret — they show you what's inside.

Change Principle: Events never define us — they always reveal us.

When life presses on you, what's on the inside comes out. If you find yourself angry or afraid, that just means anger and fear were already in there. When grace and faith and peace appear — they were also inside.

First reactions show us what's on the inside, because events never define us; they always reveal us. This principle or guide serves you by showing you exactly where you are, and that is where the journey always begins.

Milestone 1: Confront yourself with facts.

Denial is like receiving your travel itinerary and refusing to admit you are taking a trip. You don't pack, you don't plan, and you don't prepare. The lack of preparation doesn't change the fact that you are going somewhere. It does mean you may end up going without what you need, and you may get lost along the way. A trip like that is full of detours, back roads, and anxiety.

The first goal when faced by change is to confront yourself with facts. Ask yourself:

"What do I know about this situation?"

"What do I need to find out before I draw any conclusions?"

Gathering facts around you is very useful because denial can't sit comfortably alongside facts, and emotion can't walk next to logic. It's important to stick with the facts, not your interpretations, assumptions, or judgments.

Suppose you work in a department that is experiencing real productivity and quality issues. Today you've learned a new employee has been hired. This new employee is very experienced. In fact, this individual has more experience than you. What is your first emotional reaction?

Some people respond to this example in very confident, productive ways. "Great," they say, "I need the help!" Many people respond to the uncertainty of the situation. They wonder what this means. Am I being replaced or passed over? Has my boss lost confidence in my ability? Will this person outperform me? Am I at risk?

Think about your own situation for a moment.

If you allow fear and denial to speak, what do they say?

On the other hand, what are the simple facts?

What do you need to know in order to be effective?

When you shift from the emotional reaction to the logic of the situation, you have taken an important first step. You've suspended judgments and silenced denial. This can be very difficult because sometimes the facts aren't pleasant. You may face uncomfortable or even painful realities.

Change Principle: In change, truth is more important than good news.

In our example, you may have to acknowledge that you do need help. You might have to admit that you've been "asleep at the wheel." You weren't aware of how far results have slipped off the track. Denying the facts will not make you more effective — it will make you reactionary.

No matter how difficult it is to face, in change, truth is more important than good news. This guide directs you to the next principle of change — you will most likely find that you do not have everything you need to make this trip.

Change Principle: When you are called to change, equip yourself for the journey.

Change will always require something new of you. What got you where you are, won't take you one step further. You'll need new skills, new perspectives, and new approaches. You'll need people too — people who have been this way before — people who can see further down the road. When you are called to change, equip yourself with the tools and relationships you need to move forward.

This principle also speaks to pro-activity. You dramatically increase change-ability by constantly taking personal inventory, upgrading your skills, and building relationships. You "dig your wells before you're thirsty."

Has change ever caught you by surprise? You didn't see it coming and then there it was. Turn up your awareness. What is changing in your industry and your organization? What is changing in your relationships? How are you changing?

Expect change to be coming around the next corner. It is coming. Will you be ready to maximize the opportunity? As you confront the facts and increase your awareness, you have reached an important milestone. You are ready to take the next step.

Milestone 2: Empower yourself and others.

People tend to search for evidence to support what they already believe to be true. If I initially see change as a threat, I will begin gathering evidence to support that theory. Have you ever purchased a car, and leaving the lot, you begin to notice every car like yours? Do you think those cars weren't there before? Of course they were! You just weren't looking for them.

In the same way, if I view the new employee as a threat to my security and position, how will it affect my interactions with that person? I might look for flaws and point out mistakes. In the worst-case scenario, I might even sabotage or undermine the new person.

The second stage of change, resistance, is like that. It is noticing everything that supports your initial emotional reaction. Resistance builds a case against change, it looks for flaws, places blame, and behaves like a victim.

"This will never work."

"They don't pay me enough to put up with this."

"Management is clueless."

"This isn't fair."

Resistance has another voice — it criticizes you.

"I can't do this."

"This is all my fault."

I've met people who are stuck in resistance. They are exhausted with their efforts to push change back and maintain the status quo. In all of that struggling, they have not managed to stop change, they have changed after all. They have changed into someone who is bitter, angry, and hopeless. I've learned from them that it is possible to grow or wither inside of change.

The goal is to transform resistance into empowerment. Look for ways to empower yourself and others. The obstacle you face in making this transformation is often one of focus.

Change Principle: We move through change more effectively when we focus on what we can control.

Especially in times of change, there is a natural tendency to focus on what we do not control — on what is happening to us. If I allow myself to focus on what I can't change, I give my power away. I become a victim of the circumstance, allowing events to control my actions and reactions. In that way, I am tossed about by every wind and wave.

This guide encourages you to move through change more effectively by focusing on what you can control.

"What is the action I can take?"

"What is the impact I can have?"

"What is the difference I can make?"

The moment you shift your focus to that which you can control, you empower yourself. And you can empower others in the same way. You become a catalyst for positive change when you help others focus on what they can do.

Have you ever listened to someone whine and complain endlessly? This is a classic example of someone who is focused on what he or she can't control. You become the guide for others when you ask them, "What can you do to improve this situation?" Or, "How would you like this to turn out?"

Shifting your focus allows you to create positive expectations. You are no longer thinking about what might happen to you; you are thinking about what you want to happen.

Change Principle: Optimism is learned.

Another ingredient of empowerment is your internal communication or self-talk. What you say to yourself is essential because those thoughts grow into expectations, actions, and results. What you expect is what you get. Develop positive expectations and empower yourself with positive, affirming statements:

I can do this.

I am growing stronger every day.

I am valuable.

At this point of the journey, you turn the corner to see what you didn't notice before: possibility lies ahead.

Milestone 3: Find possibility.

The third stage of change is exploration. In this stage, we've accepted the change as a reality, and we're trying to find our footing. You arrive at this milestone when you move beyond acceptance and efforts to "function" in spite of the change. The guide encourages you to reach for possibility.

Change Principle: You can't reach possibility from where you are — you must step out of your comfort zone.

If you want something you've never had, you'll have to do something you've never done. Reaching for possibility means trying new things, and being willing to fail and still try again. Are you willing to stretch yourself and step out of that safe place?

Possibility thinking is a new skill for many of us. We can become pretty limited in our thinking. It takes practice to break through the limits we create in our own minds. Build this skill by thinking about your options. Brainstorm the actions you can take, and challenge your assumptions.

Remember where we began? Change is often accompanied by a sense of loss. With this turn, you begin to understand that something is to be gained. The "something gained" may be quite tangible — a new job, better health, or more money in the checking account. Again, the abstracts in life are affected — security, achievement, confidence, and self-esteem.

Apply possibility thinking to your situation:

What are you assuming about this change or about yourself?

What limits have you placed on yourself or others involved?

What step are you most afraid to take? Why?

How could you benefit from this change?

How would the most successful person you know approach this?

In between here and there, you have limitless options. Keep in mind that every choice you make will take you by a different route. It's important to have a clear destination in mind.

Change Principle: A clear destination allows you to find the most efficient path.

This guide offers age-old wisdom: set goals.

What do you value most?

What do you want?

Where do you want to end up?

What is the legacy you want to leave behind?

Your goals and values are like a compass — they direct your steps and keep you on course. Make them very specific and plan to measure your progress. Break large, long-term goals into smaller steps.

Visualize yourself achieving your goals. Actually see yourself there — being that, doing that, and having that.

Draw your map on paper, and refer to it frequently. That means write your goals down and read them every day! When you do this, something fantastic happens — you will begin to see opportunities, possibilities, and options you didn't notice before.

Milestone 4: Leverage opportunity.

The final stage of change is commitment. You have not only accepted the change, you are functioning again. This may feel like the end of the journey. It is not! Now is the moment to leverage the opportunity.

Through this change you've grown, developed essential skills, and forged new relationships. You've added value to yourself and you've appreciated as an asset to your organization. You equipped yourself for the journey and these tools will continue to serve you. Take a moment to reflect on how far you've come.

How have your perspectives changed?

What knowledge have you acquired?

What value have you added?

How can you apply what you've learned to be even more effective?

Think too about relationships. Continue to build a network of support, encouragement, and sound advice. Build your community. Make networking a high priority in your personal and professional roles.

Document your successes and communicate your results. When you market your experience and results, you open the door to new opportunities and greater levels of influence. You'll find you are now in a position to demonstrate leadership and guide others through change.

You are that person who can see farther down the road, and you are a resource for those who are just beginning their own journey. Be vigilant, like a watchperson on the wall. What changes are on the wind? Be proactive, so that you can sound the trumpet of change and lead the way.

Change is not an event, it is a process, and we are always in the process of change. Where are you now in the journey? What do you need to do to stand on the shoulders of change? What principles of change will be most helpful to you now? I encourage you to take this moment, locate yourself on the map, and build an action plan to reach the next milestone.

As you travel the paths of change, may you be blessed. May every change leave you stronger and bring you to a higher place. May you find hope in the valleys and joy on the mountains. May you be a guide for someone who has lost his or her way. And may you look back on the journey, grateful for what it made possible.

As you travel, take the map with these milestones clearly marked:

Confront yourself with facts.

Empower yourself and others.

Find possibility.

Leverage opportunity.

Grasp tightly the hands of your guides — the Principles of Change:

Events never define us — they always reveal us.

Truth is more important than good news.

When you are called to change, equip yourself for the journey.

We move through change effectively when we focus on what we can control.

Optimism is learned.

You can't reach possibility from where you are — you must step out of your comfort zone.

A clear destination allows you to find the most efficient path.

ABOUT
DONDI SCUMACI

Prior to establishing her consulting firm, Dondi Scumaci served as Vice President and Director for two major financial institutions. Dondi is an International Performance Consultant who works with individuals and organizations to enhance leadership, communication, and team building skills. She possesses a strong business and leadership background, excellent presentation skills, and a love for developing people. Through executive coaching, she assists clients in their professional development. Most often, Dondi is hired to speak at strategic design sessions, management retreats, and professional conferences. She is also a popular keynoter. Known for high energy on the platform and for the dramatic results her seminars inspire, Dondi's workshops are designed to deliver solid, actionable disciplines. She has delivered seminars in the United States, Canada, United Kingdom, Australia, and South Africa.

Contact information:
Dondi Scumaci
Elevations Unlimited, Inc.
2438 Rim Oak
San Antonio, TX 78232
Phone: (210) 545-6277
E-mail: DScumaci@ElevationsUnlimited.com
Website: www.ElevationsUnlimited.com

CHANGE: NOWHERE TO RUN, NOWHERE TO HIDE — PRACTICAL WAYS TO MASTER YOUR THINKING AND NAVIGATE THE SEA OF CHANGE

By Della Menechella

It was a change I both feared and expected. My husband's company was merging with the NASDAQ. His job had been eliminated. I changed from having a husband who was a high-level executive to having a husband who was unemployed.

One of the few things we can count on in life is constant change. Change is inevitable. Each time we begin a new aspect of our lives, we move away from what we know and are familiar with, into unknown areas and uncharted territories. New beginnings usually require that we expand outside our comfort zones.

Many of us don't like new things or change of any kind. Even if we are not thrilled with the way things are, at least we are comfortable with them and are used to them. Most of us assume that a change will put us in a worse position than our current one. We think we are going to trade in what we have now and get something worse. We don't want to take the risk that changes may bring.

When we think about change, we tend to focus on all the catastrophes that will occur because of it. On some level we fear that the change will be too difficult for us to deal with.

Change is not always an easy process. But it is possible to get through it and become stronger as a result. Change can be painful or it can be a growth process. The choice is ours.

When my husband lost his job, I realized that I could resist and resent the situation (which I was very tempted to do), or I could choose to look at it as a growth opportunity. I chose the latter because I've come to realize that when you resist change, it only makes the situation more painful, and it doesn't turn things back to the way they were. In reality, when I look back at my life, I know that I've achieved my greatest growth when I've been forced by circumstances to change.

One of the most important things that we need to focus on as we deal with change is to manage our states of mind. Whether you have lost your job and are in the process of finding a new one, or you are experiencing organizational restructuring, or you are dealing with a rapidly evolving industry, how well you manage your mindset will strongly determine how successful you will be. The people who successfully get through difficult times are the ones who are able to manage their thought processes.

We can influence our frame of mind rather than simply react to what happens on the outside. People who have mastered the ability to change their emotional state at will are more able to deal with any changing environment in which they find themselves.

Monitor Your Language

One of the key ways that we can begin to manage our thoughts and emotions is to pay attention to our language. Our words have a tremendous impact on our lives. How an individual describes a situation will make it true for him, either through what he tells others or what he tells himself. Self-talk is the continuous conversation we have with ourselves. Many people are not even aware that they engage in self-talk. So often, we don't even recognize that the voices are there, but we are acting on them anyway. Much of what we tell ourselves is negative and self-limiting. If you use negative language, you'll be tempted to give up before you even start. You need to become aware of when you are engaging in negative self-talk or when you are having pessimistic conversations with others. Only then can you make a different choice and begin to manage your state of mind.

Language is extremely important because it contributes to the beliefs that we hold. Henry Ford said, "If you think you can or you think you can't, you're right." When you start to say things like "I'll never adjust to this change," it becomes part of your belief system. Your beliefs cause you to act in ways that support that belief, and you eventually create a self-fulfilling prophecy.

Challenge your negative language, especially negative self-talk, and substitute empowering language that will allow you to look at change in a positive way. Decide to consistently use positive self-talk. Successful people use positive self-talk when they are dealing with challenges. They know their self-talk will affect how a situation will turn out for them. They tell themselves "I will find another job. I am a very capable individual and employers would be lucky to have me as an employee." "I may have a lot of projects to work on, but I will find a way to get them done on time and correctly."

You always want to tell yourself, "I will successfully handle this situation."

*Action Step — Pay attention to the negative words you say
to yourself and others. Begin to challenge your negative statements
and substitute more positive statements.*

Take Control of Your Thinking

I don't know about you, but sometimes my thoughts seem to go off and running in a direction of their own choosing. I begin to imagine catastrophes of every kind descending upon me and that I will be unable to move past them. Sometimes the thoughts are so powerful, I feel defeated before I even attempt to try to act on a good idea. When I let it run free, this line of thinking puts me in a very bad state.

We need to decide to take control of our thoughts during challenging times. Many people believe they are at the mercy of their thinking but that is not true. We make very strong decisions in other areas of our lives, but we often don't assert our power over our thoughts. Think about a food that you really hate, something that you would not eat under any circumstances. If I put it in front of you and asked you to eat it, you would probably say, "No way. I am not eating that. Never in a million years." You would have no problem making a firm decision in that situation. Why not assert that same firmness when it comes to negative thinking? When a negative thought comes to you, pretend it is that despised food being offered to you and say, "No way. I am not allowing any of that into my mind." Your mind will respond to your decision, and that thought will not find its way in.

Sport Some Rose-Colored Glasses

Life is neutral. Things are neither good nor bad, they just are. William Shakespeare said, "There is nothing either good or bad but thinking makes it so." Our perception or judgment of an event determines its meaning to us. The meaning we attach to any event affects how we feel about it.

James Allen, author of *As A Man Thinketh,* said, "A man cannot choose his circumstances, but he can choose his thoughts and so indirectly, yet surely, shape his circumstances." We cannot necessarily control what happens in our lives; however, we do have the ability to interpret every situation in a way that enables us to move forward.

Last year, I had to change my health insurance plan because my husband's COBRA had expired. I finally signed up for a new plan but it didn't include dental coverage, and I was too busy to investigate possible dental plans. As luck would have it, I developed an acute and severe infection in my gum that required immediate oral surgery. The nurse told me that the surgery would cost $1,000. I was furious with myself because I had not gotten new dental insurance. I was in a terrible state. Then I remembered that when we did have dental coverage, I once had a co-payment of $1,200 for a procedure. I decided to consider the $1,000 as a co-payment. As soon as I perceived the amount in a different way, I felt better and was able to concentrate on my work. Some people might say that it was only semantics and I still had to pay the money. While they are correct that the financial impact was the same, they are not correct about the emotional impact. One description of the situation caused me to feel anger and frustration, and the other interpretation allowed me to experience a sense of peace.

You can look at a lost job as an opportunity to find a better job somewhere else. You can consider changes at work as an opportunity to show others more of your talents and to learn new skills. It doesn't matter whether or not other people agree with your interpretation of the situation. It only matters if you feel more able to effectively handle the situation.

Action Step — Look at those areas in your life that you've interpreted in a negative way. Describe them in a way that puts you into a positive state of mind.

Look for the Pony

Many of you have heard the story about the young boy who finds himself surrounded by a huge pile of horse manure. Instead of being upset, he is beaming. When asked about his unusual reaction to this heap he replied, "With all this manure there must be a pony in here somewhere."

Adopt the attitude of this young boy and look for the pony. When you find yourself in a changing situation, look for what's positive in it. Don't ask yourself "Why did this happen?" "What are we going to do?" These are not very proactive questions, and they will usually cause you to end up in a negative loop that only makes you feel worse about the situation. Instead, ask yourself "What's good about this?" "What is of value here?" "How can this serve me?" If you ask yourself these questions, your brain will continue to search until it finds an answer.

Very often we find that we resist trying to come up with anything positive about the change. Tell yourself "I know I feel that there is nothing good in this situation, but if I could find something positive, what would it be?" You can train your brain to search for the value. If you look hard enough at any situation, you can find something positive about it.

During my husband's downsizing experience, he ended up being unemployed for two years except for two long consulting assignments. Last year he received a job offer from a company, but the salary was significantly lower than what he had previously earned. In addition, in his former position he was a corporate vice president with 100 people reporting to him, while this job was at a manager's level with only six people reporting to him. To say that my husband and I were upset and discouraged is an understatement. We were miserable for days because he needed to work, but we were very unhappy with the salary aspect of this job. We decided to look for the good in it (which I must admit was a major challenge). We came up with several positives. The job was close to our home instead of a three-hour round trip to Wall Street. It involved negotiating billion dollar contracts, which is something that my husband enjoyed doing. The company was growing at the rate of 30 percent per year so there were potential opportunities for bigger jobs in the future. The company paid a bonus and awarded stock options, which could amount to significant financial compensation. They offered a full benefits package, which meant that I did not have to pay for them out of my business. When we were able to look at the positives in the situation, my husband took the job.

When something happens that causes a change in our lives, we have the choice to moan, groan, and complain about it, but those reactions don't change the reality of the situation. By focusing on the good, we are usually able to transform our attitudes into something more positive, which helps us get through the situation more effectively.

Action Step — *Come up with some positives about your situation.*

Consider the Lesson

Every situation in which we find ourselves has a lesson for us that can contribute to our success in the future. Sometimes people find themselves in the same or similar situations over and over again because they don't heed the lesson. If we learn what we need to learn, we can become better prepared to meet the future.

A number of years ago my husband and I owned a contract cleaning service. Our business had high and low periods, with the winter being a particularly slow time. We obtained a contract for year-round cleaning of a 90,000-square-foot conference center that helped us get through the winter months. We had this client for more than four years and expected this contract to continue indefinitely because we provided outstanding service, and we also enjoyed a very good relationship with the executives of the center. Then the unthinkable happened. The economy had shifted sufficiently downward so that the general manager had to cancel our contract and take the cleaning services in-house. A substantial portion of our business disappeared overnight. We had become comfortable and had not tried to diversify our customer base. As a result we had to scramble to try to recoup some of the revenues. We learned that, no matter how wonderful the relationship is between you and a client, it can be financial suicide to put all your proverbial eggs in one basket when it comes to revenues.

Action Step — What have you learned from your current experience with change? How can this be useful to you in the future?

Mine Your Resources

Each of us has many internal resources that we often do not use when we could most benefit from them. Many people believe that they can use the resource in one context but not in another. If you have ever experienced a positive state of mind, it is coded into your nervous system, and you can access that state and use it when it can be of value to you. For instance, someone may be confident in his ability to handle a social situation but not feel confident in his ability to handle change. If an individual knows how to feel confident socially, then he has the ability to experience the state of confidence and he can use it to help him effectively handle change.

We want to use positive emotions at those times when we need them most. Then we move away from being reactive to our environment and begin to choose what we want to experience. Think about a state of mind that could be beneficial to you during a time of transition. Now remember a specific time in your life when you have felt this particular emotion. Relive this positive experience in detail. What did you see? What did you hear inside your mind and outside? How did you feel? What was your breathing like? How were you holding your body? Allow yourself to relive this experience in great detail so that the emotion is fully present in your body. Now think about when it would be useful for you to feel this emotion in the future.

This process was tremendously valuable to me several years ago after I lost my father-in-law to cancer. Three days after he died I was scheduled to present a program to several hundred people. I was stricken with overwhelming grief. If I had spoken to the group while I was in that state of mind, it would have been a dismal experience for all of us. Before I gave my speech I remembered a time in the past when I had really been 'on.' I relived that experience fully in my mind. When it was time for me to start my talk, I was my typical high-energy, enthusiastic self, and it turned out to be a wonderful time for all.

Action Step — Think about positive emotions that could be resources for you. Go back to times in your past when you have felt those emotions and relive those experiences. Access these positive emotions before you deal with challenging situations.

Create a New Vision for Yourself

You also want to create a vision of the way that you want your life to be. The pictures you create in your head contribute to your state of mind. Albert Einstein said, "Imagination is more important than knowledge." Creating a positive image of what you want to achieve helps you to focus your energies. It also helps you to get past the setbacks that may occur on a periodic basis. Instead of getting stuck in the setbacks, you can look to your vision to help you move forward.

Whatever we focus on in life, we get more of. If we focus on the day-to-day difficulties, we will find ourselves having more difficulties to face. However, if we focus on the way we want our lives to be, we will begin to attract that which we envision.

If you are looking for a new job, see yourself working in a wonderful position, earning a terrific salary, and having a great time. If things are in transition in your organization, see yourself managing all of your work easily and efficiently and enjoying what you are doing.

The great American psychologist William James said, "Your vision is your promise of what you shall one day be." Create a vision in your mind of what you want to experience. If you start to continually imagine yourself acting as if your vision were true, then you will automatically start to behave that way.

Action Step — *Write a detailed description of what you would like to experience as a result of your new situation. Play this picture over and over in your mind.*

Turn to Faith

Sometimes a change occurs in our lives that is of such magnitude that even the strongest of us cannot seem to summon the strength to get through it. As I sit and write this, it has been almost a week since the horrific attack on the World Trade Center in New York and the Pentagon in Washington, D.C. Thousands of people were killed, businesses were devastated, and families and friends of the victims have had their lives irreparably altered in the most tragic way. During those times in our lives when we are paralyzed with fear and grief by terrible events, it helps to turn to our personal faith that something much greater than we are will carry us through. When you find yourself in a situation that overwhelms you, you can turn to your personal Higher Power to help restore you to wholeness.

Change is not an easy process. However, we can make it easier or more difficult by how we decide to react to it. Willow trees bend with the wind; they go with the flow. They do not try to stand up against the forces of a hurricane and they usually survive. On the other hand, oak trees can be torn apart by the forces of a hurricane because they are rigid, and they try to resist the wind. It's the same with change. If we say no to change and play the role of victims, change can be very painful. If we say yes to change, we can let go of the resistance, go with the flow of events, and take advantage of the incredible opportunities that change frequently brings.

ABOUT
DELLA MENECHELLA

*D*ella Menechella is a professional speaker and peak performance consultant who specializes in presenting lectures and workshops that help attendees achieve greater success in both their personal and professional lives. Della spent ten years as a corporate human resources executive for Viacom where she implemented a variety of programs which resulted in increased employee performance. She has been a successful entrepreneur for ten years and is the creator of the videotape "The Twelve Commandments of Goal Setting." Della is a certified Master Practitioner of Neuro-Linguistic Programming, a model of communications excellence, and she has spent the last sixteen years researching the details of success and peak performance strategies. This unique combination of experience and knowledge allows Della to create and present programs that result in higher levels of individual performance. Some of the results of Della's programs include higher productivity, improved morale, higher sales closing ratios, more effective leadership, a greater ability to deal with change, and higher levels of individual and team performance. Her clients include American Express, Johnson & Johnson, and Exxon.

Contact information:
Della Menechella
Personal Peak Performance Unlimited
8 Carmello Drive
Edison, NJ 08817
Phone: (732) 985-1919
Fax: (732) 572-2941
E-mail: Menech@DellaMenechella.com
Website: www.DellaMenechella.com

Customer Focus: How One Doctor Challenged a Changing System and Won — And What You Can Do in Your Business with What You Learn!

by Louis B. Cady, M.D.

The idea of a psychiatrist writing a chapter on customer service, in a book on *change*, is, at first blush, counter-intuitive. One stereotyped view of psychiatrists is that of some bearded "Dr. Freudy" type guy sitting behind a psychoanalytic couch and just mumbling "umh humh." A more contemporary, and far more realistic, view for patients who have actually seen a modern psychiatrist is that of some sort of mental health care provider in a monolithic bureaucratic HMO. In this iteration, we're just a bunch of guys and gals who talk to people all day, write prescriptions, and pretty much do things the same way we always have. Change is certainly not part of the world view in either one of these mental pictures.

The ignorance of change by practitioners, both in psychiatry and in medicine in general, is ironic and tragic because change is decimating psychiatry and forcing untold pain and misery on physicians, therapists, and most importantly, their patients. Put succinctly, ignorance of the driving forces of change — coupled with a lack of focused, targeted, and viscerally understood principles of customer service — has increasingly made the provision of quality mental health care services disintermediated and extinct. The same will happen to you and your business if you are not aware of the forces of change and if you do not have a deep and abiding respect for the principles of excellent customer service.

A broad understanding of the driving forces of change, coupled with a focused, targeted, deeply held commitment to customer service, will allow you to do the following:

- charge more than the competition (much more)

- change the rules of the game to the way that you want to play

- develop such a high-demand service that people will stand in line and wait months for the privilege and the opportunity to do business with you. They will also not blink an eye when it is time to pay.

Let's get one thing straight about credibility: the words you are reading are the way I live my life and run my business. Like a straight commission salesperson, if I don't see patients, and if they don't pay me, I don't eat and my family doesn't eat. Nobody guarantees my income. I don't accept Medicare, Medicaid, or insurance assignment. I accept cash, check, or charge. Hardly anyone runs a psychiatric practice like that these days because hardly anyone knows how. The profession of psychiatry, as well as medicine in general, has lost its grip on what it means to deliver a good service for a good fee. Meddling interlopers, managed care bureaucrats, reviewers, and health maintenance organizations have all come between physicians and patients with siren songs. To physicians, they sing, "We will guarantee you a certain income per year, but you've got to see who we say, when we say, for as short a period of time as we say, and, if you do that, we will continue to pay you." The implied corollary is, "Even if you aren't doing what you like, with whom you like, and serving your patients as you feel you should, that's too bad because this is the bargain you made."

To patients, the siren song is, "Pay us our monthly premium and your health care will be free, free, free!" The unspoken corollary is, "Yes, and you will go to see who we say, when we say, for as long as we say, and you will like it."

And physicians, in a neurotic compromise of passive acceptance, sadly sing, "Que sera, sera — whatever will be, will be."

This is socialism. My practice is the antithesis of it — and your business should be as well.

My enlightenment did not come overnight. But I did have two advantages going into the practice of medicine. The first advantage was that I actually had run a successful business before graduating from medical school. The fact that it was a piano tuning business, of all things, was even more useful! I found that if I delivered an excellent product, for a fair fee, and educated my customers and guaranteed their satisfaction, I would never have to advertise and would constantly have word-of-mouth referrals. I did this all the way through medical school. When I closed my business, I was charging fifty percent more than any of my competition and I still had a waiting list. Very few physicians have had that type of free-market, capitalistic background.

The second advantage was that I had read, believed, and determined to practice Zig Ziglar's aphorism that, "You can have everything in life you want if you just help enough other people get what they want."

When I finished residency, because I was the typical post-educated-strapped-for-cash physician, I accepted a contracted position with a hospital. This was, at the time, a useful and positive experience. I decided that since someone else was guaranteeing my income, I would use the experience as a learning laboratory. The worst that could happen is that there would be insufficient professional fees coming in and I would be told to change my ways; the best that could happen is that a novel and much more profitable style of practice that would keep the hospital happy could be developed. The second possibility is what transpired.

Here is how I did it:

- I defined my product: *To provide excellent, humane, empathic, caring psychiatric services with a guarantee that I would not turn people into zombies or waste their money.*

- I marketed my product by a number of free, public, educational seminars.

- I determined that I was going to give extraordinary customer service. This included a "twenty minutes or it's free" guarantee where patients did not have to wait, the provision of multiple pieces of educational material about my practice and practice philosophy so patients would feel like they knew me before they even walked through the door, and a careful explanation of fees and how they would be collected. I also did something exceptionally radical in the medical profession. I gave a "risk reversal guarantee." Basically, it went like this, "If you're not happy at the end of your appointment, if you don't feel like you've been treated with respect, or that your questions have not been answered, or if you're just dissatisfied in any respect, simply tell my office manager and you won't owe me a dime. If you are satisfied, however, then we'll expect payment."

- Other small touches included a video game system for my child patients to use in a separate room while I chatted with their parents, as well as free soft drinks for kids and parents when they came to visit.

- I banned all magazines older than three months from my waiting room area and subscribed to a diverse assortment of publications so that all my patients could find something to read that was current and enjoyable.

Basically, for five years as an employed physician, my business exploded and I had the highest collection rate of any psychiatrist in the group. My patients paid their bills because they were satisfied, and they knew what the deal was when they arrived on my doorstep.

Mutual dissatisfaction with the hospital that employed me evolved over the last two years of my contract, and I severed our relationship and went totally solo. The hospital was sold out and ceased to exist — because of poor customer service. My practice has become even more exciting and rewarding, and my patients even more loyal — because of good customer service.

Let's get down to some real numbers:

- In my first 37 months of solo private practice, starting with zero income and opening the doors on July 15, 1998, I took in, "cash on the barrel head," over one million dollars of gross income.

- My receivables run at a tiny fraction of that, around 3 percent.

- People are willing to wait four to six months to be seen for new appointments. (I try to work emergencies in sooner than that.)

- I have to give my established and stable patients scheduled appointments "every three or four months" for up to one year in advance in order to insure that there will be room to accommodate them.

- My practice is the only one in the region that is not a hostage to managed care. I set my own hours, my own fees, and see whom I want, when I want, where I want. And my patients are delighted with this arrangement!

How have I done it? Customer service is the answer.

My definition of customer service is providing the customer with the optimum product to meet his or her needs, at a fair price, in an excellent way. These principles of good customer service do not vary, whether you're shrinking heads, making and selling widgets, or selling shoes. Customer service is, in this view, not what you say, but what you do and how you are with people.

To review these concepts, let's take a look at three different situations and relate them to customer service, to what I did, and to what you may be doing.

When my family and I moved across town to a different subdivision, a very nice man came by and offered to do our lawn. Truly, he did a magnificent job. I was well pleased with the quality of his work. Then a neighbor boy came by and offered to cut our yard for half as much. Basically, I chose the neighbor boy because of the price. The service was the same, the quality was about the same, but the price was half. All other things being equal, price always wins.

Second story. I have my hair cut at a nice salon in our local shopping mall. One gentleman who cut it was very pleasant, did a very good job, and charged a fair price. I always asked for him. One evening when he wasn't there, a new stylist, Sherry, was assigned to me. She sized up my hair with the cool appraising eye of an expert, told me that when she got finished it would lie perfectly, and then proceeded to give me the best hair cut I've ever had. I frankly don't remember if the cost was a couple dollars more or not; what impressed me was that it was a stunningly good job. I started asking for Sherry after that. On one occasion, the gentleman who had previously cut my hair was sitting at the front of the salon waiting for another customer as I walked in for my appointment with Sherry. He looked up, startled, knowing that I had asked for somebody other than him. I could read the look of surprise and hurt in his eyes as he recognized that he had lost me as a customer. While I felt sorry for him, I did what any enlightened customer would have done: price being roughly equal, I chose the best quality I could get.

Third story. A few psychiatrists that I know are aware of the type of practice that I run. Recently, through a mutual friend, I got an inquiry from one of them asking if his office manager could talk with mine about the forms we use to insure good collections. It was an interesting request. I personally authored every word of the forms that my practice uses, and they spell out the entire practice philosophy. I agreed to let this other practice review one of my forms, but did so somewhat regretfully, recognizing that unless this office totally remodels the financial structure of its own practice and changes its underlying philosophy, the forms I provided to them will be useless.

Here's the deal. Customer service starts before the sale. It starts by defining what you are going to offer, to whom, and at what price. This paradigm includes a clear mental picture of your ideal practice or business situation. Only at the "delivery of services stage" does customer service encompass how you are going to offer your service or product. In this sense, customer service is not something you "do" or "manage" after you put your business in place. It is your business. It is integral to the conception and design of your business. And if it's not in place, please let me suggest some urgent remodeling!

For my practice, it starts by defining the buying criteria, and of "de-widgetizing" me. Psychiatrists these days are known as providers. As such, bureaucratic managed care organizations consider one provider the same as any other provider: basically, as interchangeable widgets. Dr. Widget, M.D., is replaceable with other interchangeable widgets in the minds of the bureaucrats

Key point: if your customers don't know what separates you or your business from any other of your competitors, you're just a widget . . . just like my lawn care providers were widgets. In "widget-to-widget" competition, price always wins.

There are several ways in which I have grown my practice to become "de-widgetized." First is my reputation, which I've built on numerous public lectures, creative marketing ideas, and the delivery of excellent care. The more discombobulated and out of control the adult or munchkin-sized patient who comes in, the more dramatic and miraculous are the results when I get them stabilized. Satisfied patients represent my public relations army. Satisfied customers can represent yours!

Secondly, when patients call for an appointment, the first thing they receive is a very interesting document. The first part of it describes all of the customer service guarantees that I offer; the second part basically demands that they sign the form, acknowledging that they understand that they will be expected to pay at the conclusion of the appointment if they are satisfied. This form makes clear to prospective patients that I will not bill insurance companies and then wait (and hope!) to be paid. It therefore eliminates any misunderstandings right up front.

Note carefully the order of the document: the first part states what I am going to do for them. That's a service orientation. The second part emphasizes their responsibility to me. Most people understand that relationship. But many businesses get this process reversed and start thinking about what they are going to get from the customer first. Profits! Sales! Then only as a sort of incidental afterthought do they consider what they are going to provide: service. It is this backwards paradigm that inevitably ends with difficulties.

So what are the customer service guarantees that motivate people to sign my forms acknowledging that they are going to actually have to pay with some of their hard-earned money rather than expect their insurance or their managed care plan to provide them a "free" mental health service? Try these on for size:

- You will be seen on time or it's FREE.

- You will be treated with respect.

- I will not turn you into some sort of drugged zombie. Side effects from medications are not acceptable.

- If you have an emergency, I will be available to you 24/7, 365 days a year — not some "on call physician" who doesn't have a clue about who you are or what your issues are.

- You won't pay after your initial appointment unless you're happy.

- I'm not going to turn you into a professional psychiatric patient. Seeing me and thinking about your mental health condition should represent an exceptionally small part of your conscious awareness. When I get you stable, you'll come to visit every three or four months because that's all you'll need to do. (This is contrasted with the psychiatric widget factories where the physician sees the patient "every month to check on your medications.")

What's not to like about this? Believe me when I tell you, no other physician — at least, none that I know of — sends out a form like this with these types of guarantees. It's interesting to note that a psychiatric practice based in Seattle, WA, charges a $13,200 per year retainer for patients to have a physician available to them 24 hours per day, 365 days per year. My patients get it as part of their typical fee, for no extra charge! From my reading, the Seattle-based practice has no shortage of patients willing to pay for their service — and neither do I. Here's a question for you: What type of service could you offer your customers that would enable you to charge this type of premium, or to justify an appropriate increase in your prices?

Back to my forms. After the patient or financial guarantor signs these forms and sends them back, a six-page personalized, hand-signed letter to the patient in my "New Patient Packet" goes out. In addition to the usual intake forms for patients to fill out, I include a copy of my "10 Commandments of Psychiatric Practice," a tri-fold on my practice philosophy, and another tri-fold to educate the patient about the "fun and games" of the insurance companies. Information on medications and an invitation to surf on by my website are also furnished. All of this comes to the patient in a high-quality, presentation folder, with an appointment card placed neatly in a window display in the folder. (All of these documents are available for review on my website at www.drcady.com.) Most of my new patients come in, clutching this folder to their chests as almost a psychiatric security blanket to reassure themselves at their first appointment.

In all of the forms that I send out, I continually emphasize a number of key points:

- I acknowledge that patients are placing their trust and faith in me, and that while I appreciate it, I think it is fundamentally unfair for them to have to assume the unfair and unequal part of a relationship in which they will get stuck with the bill at the end of the appointment, whether they're happy with the service or not.

- Patients are assured that their questions will be answered, and that any medications I use will not be prescribed in a way to waste their money or give them side effects.

- I reemphasize that they will be seen on time, every time, or it's free.

- If there ever is a problem, or if an emergency occurs, they can get in touch with me — either in town or anywhere in the country on my pager or cell phone, day or night. (You would be amazed at how infrequently this happens. When it does, it's almost always appropriate and I'm happy to take the call or page and to be able to render service. My availability generates an incredible amount of goodwill and trust.)

- I inform the patient of the amount of continuing medical education I do to keep up with the current literature.

- The patient is invited to my website, which is chock full of interesting and relevant mental health links as well as a "mental health bookstore" where further reading material and/or audiotapes can be obtained.

Many — if not all — of my medical and mental health colleagues have, unfortunately, forgotten that the practice of their profession is basically a service business! A business must make a profit in order to stay in existence. The free market system guarantees that good businesses will survive and make a profit, and undisciplined, unethical, and slipshod businesses will go under. With the interposed layers of bureaucracy between when the patient actually has to dip into his/her pocket and pay the insurance company, and then when the insurance company sometimes pays the typical physician, the correlation between performance and pay oftentimes gets indistinct. In my practice, the correlation is crystal clear: If I don't deliver the service, the patient will be unwilling to reach into his or her pocket and pay me, won't consider me a good value for the money, and I will go bankrupt. That's reality.

It's reality in your business, too. Don't get lulled into a sense of complacency if you're not a psychiatrist or physician and think, "I don't have to worry about that layer of bureaucracy and insurance company garbage." If anything — be it interposed layers of management between you and your customer, lack of surveillance of your employees and monitoring of how you and they are doing, narcissistic indifference on your part (thinking nobody could possibly top you or your product), or whatever — your lack of awareness may be even higher than the disconnected physician! If you are out of touch with what your customer thinks of you or what your competition is doing, and if you lose sight of the absolute, direct connection between keeping the customer happy (and then, in return, getting his money for the service), then your business is in danger.

Ironically, psychiatrists (and other mental health therapists), who are supposed to be the experts in understanding how people think and emote, are stunningly uncreative in the way they conceptualize their prospective patients. By the way — how are you doing on this?

For example, although mental health experts know the conditions of depression, anxiety, personality disorders, and the like, very little thought seems to be given to trying to make the patient comfortable for his or her first appointment. The risk has historically always been on the patient. It goes like this:

- You, or your insurance, will pay whether or not you like the service.
- I will do nothing to reassure you before you come to see me.
- I will not make any effort to educate you on what your expectations should be.
- I will provide only the bare minimum of services because I have chosen not to price my services at a fee where I can make a decent profit.

Also, these supposed experts into the workings of the human mind never seem to get around to asking themselves these questions:

- What am I doing to take outstanding care of my patient/customer?
- Do I have the right to charge the fees I'm asking?
- Am I worth the money?
- What evidence do I have to support that?

- Are there other things I could be doing, or other services I could be providing, to make things better for my patients?

Interestingly, if you review the previous two paragraphs and bullet-point lists and insert "CPA" or "attorney" or "financial planner" into the above scenarios, you get a similar sense of the wide-open possibilities to improve the focus on customer service in almost all professions and businesses!

One of the things that I do in my practice is ask myself, while doing psychotherapy with a patient, "Would I pay me more than $250 an hour to talk to me?" The answer to this, so far, has always been, "Yes!" There are several things I do to monitor myself and make sure I'm honestly earning my fee. Am I making good eye contact? Are my notes complete enough that I can recreate the relevant points from my memory when I dictate the session later? Am I keeping pace with the patient, rephrasing and reflecting back to the patient what is being said so I am certain that I got what the patient was saying? (What about you? What are you or your business doing to justify your fees or prices?)

In psychotherapy, all issues ultimately reduce to a conversation between the patient and the therapist. In business, all issues ultimately reduce to the dialogue between the customer and the front-line provider of the service. Stanley Greben, in a startling article published in the *British Journal of Psychiatry,* titled "On Being Therapeutic," noted that the best therapists get their results because of their deep ability to empathize with their patients and see things from the patient's point of view. Psychiatric patients, like other customers, can sometimes be irrational, demanding, and exasperating. But our ability to see things from *their* point of view — their insecurities, the lack of specific data points to make decisions, their confusion — can ultimately allow us to have the privilege of healing service, either professionally or vocationally.

I like what Dr. William Mayo, M.D. had to say in 1935 about this service orientation toward patients: "Perhaps the ability not only to acquire the confidence of the patient, but to deserve it, to see what the patient desires and needs, comes through the sixth sense we call intuition, which in turn comes from wide experience and deep sympathy for and devotion to the patient, giving to the possessor remarkable ability to achieve results."

Ultimately, whether it's selling widgets, professional services, factoring, distributing, consulting, professional speaking, or whatever, it's the level and depth of our experience in our field, and the level of deep sympathy and devotion toward our customers that will make us or break us. And perhaps even more profoundly, it is the human connection with our patients or customers that makes what we are doing more worthwhile and offers a deeper and richer appreciation of the meaning of our existence.

ABOUT
LOUIS B. CADY, M.D.

*D*r. *Louis Cady, M.D., practices child, adolescent, adult, and forensic psychiatry in Evansville, Indiana. After obtaining his medical degree in 1989, he trained in psychiatry at the Mayo Clinic. He has a diverse background as a musician and as an entrepreneur. Dr. Cady has combined his life experiences in business and medicine to acquire cutting-edge marketing and positioning skills, making his independent practice of psychiatry a remarkable success in an era of managed care. In addition to his professional practice of psychiatry, Dr. Cady has become a monthly columnist, author or contributing author of three books, and a sought-after speaker, lecturer, and consultant. A member of the National Speakers Association, Dr. Cady travels widely as a presenter for four international pharmaceutical companies and has served as an adviser, speaker, motivator, and consultant to many more area and regional businesses.*

Contact information:
Louis B. Cady, M.D.
611 Harriet Street, Suite 304
Doctors Plaza
Evansville, IN 47710
Phone: (812) 429-0772
Fax: (812) 429-0793
E-mail: LCady@DrCady.com
Website: www.DrCady.com

GOING, GROWING, OR LIVING IN A CAGE — YOU DO HAVE CHOICES!

by MaryAnn Morton

Life is full of changes and few things remain stable.
Stability does not mean lack of change, but the ability
to remain stable in the midst of things changing.

I listened as the young woman kept speaking with what seemed to be a never-ending repetition of frustration and stress. I was almost exhausted myself, just listening. Only listening, because her continual talking hardly left enough space between the words to take a breath. From experience I realized she wasn't really seeking advice, for she was totally absorbed in herself and her problems. She was stuck in her apparent life-long patterns of thinking and talking. The concept of anything other than her current, stressful circumstances would be of no value to her, including reasons to accept and adjust to the changes over which she felt she had no control. To try to show her methods and reasons for change would be futile. Her perspective, mindset, and habits of reacting prohibited her from possible solutions. To offer suggestions was not going to be beneficial, for her or myself. I had tried too many times before, giving advice when it wasn't really wanted, even though advice had been asked for. Now was a time for me to make a change and keep quiet. Because of the large amount of energy it takes to be so upset, she slowly wound down. Understandably, she appeared more tired and frustrated than when she had started. I told her I hoped things would change, knowing that unless she herself made changes within her thinking patterns, the next time I saw her nothing would be different. As I walked away, I was sadly reminded of a grasshopper caught in a cage, exerting tremendous energy and effort to get out, but going nowhere, as the sides of its cage contained it. Why do some people seem to have a more difficult time "growing" through change? Maybe you have people you work with or family members that just don't appear to grow at all. They are the people who seem to just exist through life and its challenges, instead of growing through them. The atmosphere they create and their attitude make that quite clear. Instead of ten years of experience and growth, they have repeated the same pattern ten different times, each year the same. Even though this person may not change, the frustration of dealing with this kind of situation can often be lessened if we will learn to recognize thinking patterns that contribute to reactive and response habits.

Three Kinds of Changes

There are basically three different kinds of change. The first are those that generally keep us on stable ground. These keep us within our comfort zone, even though they may cause us some emotional or physical movement and lead us into unfamiliar territory. As change is not always negative, these new experiences can often be pleasurable. A new marriage, a new home, children starting school, a new job you have wanted, a move in your current job situation, taking up a new sport, attending a new church, and even purchasing a new car. Other times, these changes may be viewed as rather small, irritating interruptions. Sometimes the change is only because of necessity and therefore may be unwelcome. Regardless, you are still willing to make those adjustments and changes because they do not create an overly large amount of lasting pressure or a feeling of loss of control.

The second kind of change is the kind that "ripples the water."

These changes have enough movement to make them somewhat interesting or even exciting because of the challenges they present. These do take you out of your comfort zone. However, the overall effect is not devastating, as you know that you can and are willing to accept and handle the change required.

The third and most difficult changes are the ones that "rock our boat" and occasionally capsize it, temporarily, we hope. Most of these catch us quite unprepared, and are totally unwelcome and unexpected. Health situations, a marriage that ends, personal circumstances, situations dealing with children or problems at work, all of which can seem disturbing and defeating day after day. Sometimes we really are in a position of being the victim or recipient of someone else's decision-making, resulting in tremendous change for us. These are often crisis moments in life. How we handle them can determine how we will live the rest of our lives, not because the effects or the situation will go away, but because of how we choose to grow through those challenging hours and days, which in turn become months and years. We can see ourselves either as a victim of change or a creator of change. We can create new change within ourselves and even reach out to influence others for a positive change, willingly or out of necessity.

"Growth Hoppers" or "Grass Hoppers"

I was raised in a home where, because of my father's vocation, I never attended one school more than two years in a row. Even though I had no choice in the decision-making for the many moves, I was forced to learn quickly how to survive in new surroundings. Not just across town, where I could still call old friends, but in new cities and states where I did not know one person. I doubt I will ever forget the feelings of anticipation each time I would walk into a new school building, find my class, and know I was definitely the "new kid on the block." As with most of us, the feeling of wanting to belong seldom goes away completely, but through necessity I soon learned to change my focus from the dread of moving and leaving friends to an excitement about new friends I would meet. The hardship, dread, and fears lessened each time as I learned that the easiest way to handle all these changes was to accept, adjust, and learn to be flexible, even though none of these moves were welcomed. Repetition often has a way of bringing us to a certain point of comfort, acceptance, denial, or decision-making, whether good or bad. I actually grew to have a sense of stability when I entered those unfamiliar buildings, wondering what new adventures awaited and always hopeful that I would surely be there at least two years and maybe longer, if I was fortunate. I now view those experiences, chosen or not, as "growth hoppers," using them to help prepare me for later changes in my life, when I have had to let go and create new patterns of thinking and behavior that would allow me to move forward.

To help establish a foundation for the ways that you currently handle change, think back to your early childhood and some changes that happened in your home environment. How did the adults in your life conduct themselves and model handling change in situations that may or may not have been pleasing for them? If you are willing to look with an open mind, you may see similar patterns in how you handle change. Our upbringing has a great deal to do with how we learn or refuse to learn how to handle life's challenging situations. We either choose to see ourselves as victims, and react accordingly, or see ourselves responsible for how we will respond, not just react, to changing circumstances. We can look at life's changes and see ourselves as small "grasshoppers," helplessly caught in a history and pattern of emotional and mental hopping around, aimlessly, or we can choose to step out of self-defeating habits and thought patterns. We can choose to create positive change. In this way, life's experiences and yes, sometimes hardships and disappointments, can become "growth hoppers" to new levels of emotional and mental maturity, allowing us to step outside the constraining cage of thinking in which we have learned to live. To help make us more conscious of resistance to the unfamiliar territory of change and lack of recognition of the power our habits have upon our life, I have written these thoughts in a different style.

"Cage Living"

I live in a cage, for
It's safe in here.
I can laugh,
Be quiet or cry.

I can't go far, but
I'm always safe, so
I adjust my wants
To its size.

I watch others pass
And still get light.
For my food?
Others throw me some crumbs.

I'm happy, secure,
No challenge, no lure.
Oh my God!
Am I brilliant or dumb?

Before you can teach yourself new habits for dealing with change, old pre-programmed patterns that are not healthy for you or those around you need to be recognized. Make a decision to let go of them. Hold on to the positive, good role models, and, at the same time, be willing to disassociate yourself from negative and destructive patterns and habits. Yes, to achieve new results you first need to have a reason and desire to create change. Make a conscious commitment to leave behind patterns of thinking, talking, and behavior that do not allow you to move ahead. Being willing to look at your current habits is the starting point for making positive change. You must decide how strongly you desire new results by deciding how much you are willing to make changes in the present. This process will enable you to step into your future with the power and strength that come from wise and deliberate decision-making.

Cage Living or Stuck in a Rut

There are many reasons people get stuck in a limited style of cage living. Many people can look back over certain periods of their life and see where they were once stuck, or certainly could have continued in the same path of familiar habits, by choosing to remain as they were. Sometimes complacency and refusal to deal with uncomfortable habits can be easier than making changes and moving forward. In a society that puts emphasis on comfort, it is easy to see why some people just refuse to deal with anything that feels different, strange, or challenging. However, the result from that decision often comes back in the form of increased stress and more tension. As anxiety is usually accompanied by some form of discomfort, this choice is self-defeating. Consider the following attitudes, which strongly contribute to living in a rut:

1. Focusing on the way things used to be.
2. Not being open to new ideas, suggestions or methods.
3. Refusal to communicate.
4. Refusal to forgive.

Each of us is involved in some kind of relationship, whether at home or at work. A person with one or more of these characteristics can be very difficult to deal with, especially if this person is your boss, a supervisor you report to, a co-worker or family member. When you are confronted by or must deal with a person such as this, remember: *you do have choices.*

Accept, Adjust, or Assertively Step Out

Many of us tend to resist change, even though we know it is good for us. We are comfortable with the known and uncomfortable with the unknown. Then there are those that seek change and welcome its challenges. Regardless of where you fit in, here are three different approaches to handling change. In addition to the following, there is one more choice, and that is to continue in an unhealthy situation, try to ignore the circumstances, and live with the stress of refusing to make any decision at all.

1. Accept: " to receive willingly, to approve, to agree, to believe in" . . .

How easy and relaxing change can be that is willingly acceptable to us. Often these kinds of changes have to do with circumstances and not people. I chuckle when I think of a counselor friend of mine who jokingly says that life would be so great if it weren't for other people. However, a tip to help you more easily cope with and accept change is to develop support relationships at work and outside of your job. People who have friends on whom they can rely during stressful times experience much less negative effects of the stress change can bring. They usually remain healthier and are able to make change a more positive experience.

2. Adjust: "change so as to fit" . . .

One method of adjusting is to change your expectations in some way, shape, or form concerning a person or situation. Be open and flexible. Realizing and accepting that change can happen helps you adjust when it occurs. Be careful of the expectations you place on another person or situation. Sometimes people will live up to your expectations, if your expectations are not self-seeking, and good will come to the other person as a result. However, if not kept in check, the same expectations can be extremely damaging, causing friction and destroying relationships. People do not always measure up to your expectations, and whether in the workplace or home, if you are unwilling to let go, you are in for trouble. Changing our expectations has a time and place and can be a real source of reason for growth in oneself. Changing expectations might be the way to add emotional stability in some of the tough relationships and situations in life. If a significant person in your life is difficult to deal with, and there is nothing you can do to make a difference in the relationship, then make a difference to yourself. Don't keep expecting what you know isn't going to happen if the same patterns are followed. Likewise, if you aren't willing to make a change and adjust, you are going to continually have the same difficulties.

3. Assertively or aggressively step out ... away from the situation entirely.

Sometimes we can eliminate an unhealthy circumstance just by assertively disassociating ourself and moving around or away from a person or situation. However, accepting or adjusting may not be an option in some instances, particularly when morals, ethics, and character are involved. Stepping out may be the wisest, most sensible decision. A quiet, assertive move might be all that is necessary to dissipate possible tension and dismiss yourself from involvement and unacceptable compromise. Other times, to step away entirely, you may need to be more aggressive and determined as to the manner in which you handle stepping out. Be careful, as this could be a very final and sometimes disruptive move. It is usually wise to be sure you have shared your consideration with someone whom you respect and who is qualified to listen. This person also needs to be qualified to recognize and share with you the possible consequences of your decision-making, which could be negative as well as positive. Decision-making because of impatience, personality differences, or unwillingness to accept and adjust needs the wisdom of timing. Do not be caught in the unfortunate situation of making a hasty decision you later regret. If possible, change what you don't like about your situation or accept what you can't change. If you can do neither, then it may be time to step out into a new direction. When considering options and opportunities, reexamine the old. What worked that you liked and what should be left behind?

The ability to learn how to respond and not just react is most important in handling change. The person who has learned this wisdom almost always has a much quieter attitude than the loud, attention-seeking, and demanding person. Sad to say, this is not learned by a certain age or position. Some people never acquire this maturity. A pattern of fast and harsh reacting usually stems from disrupted emotions and often contains words and attitudes expressed that are often later regretted. This kind of behavior seldom resolves anything and makes for additional problems and hardships, particularly in relationships. Even though circumstances and people will affect you, do not let them control you, your thoughts, or your actions. This takes concentrated and deliberate effort to instill this habit of thinking and perspective within oneself. Make an effort to stay flexible, and keep a focus on yourself, as someone you admire and respect.

Habits Recognized and Changes Needed

After carefully reading through the following, select two changes to which you are going to apply a concentrated effort for the next sixteen days. Only after you have started to see a positive change in your thinking and actions, add one more for the next sixteen days. Continue this practice and pattern of adding one at a time. Don't get discouraged. After you are willing to let go of old habits, it still takes time to create new.

GRASS HOPPER HABITS

1. I speak before thinking.
2. I give opinions without firsthand information.
3. I am easily offended.
4. I take too much personally.
5. I am insulted too easily.
6. I resist new methods and ideas, especially if I didn't think of them.
7. I am defensive when given suggestions about something I am doing.
8. I do not listen well. I am thinking of my reply while someone else is speaking to me.
9. I usually talk the most during conversation with someone else.
10. I interrupt others to express my opinion.
11. I exaggerate truths, making my words less valuable.
12. I am uncomfortable with silence in a conversation. As a result, I automatically continue or start talking to fill the silence.

GROWTH HOPPER CHANGES

1. Pause and think a few seconds before speaking.

2. Refrain from always giving your opinion.

3. Let go of it. If possible, remove yourself from the offending person or situation.

4. Consider if there is truth and overlook the rest.

5. Don't let others' words and actions determine yours.

6. Learn value in listening to what you haven't thought of.

7. Learn to say, "Thanks for the suggestion." Quietly consider it. Don't let pride rob you of possible improvement.

8. Discipline yourself to really listen. Listen from your heart, not just your head.

9. Practice the art of talking the least in a conversation. Learn not to tell everything you know (or think you know).

10. Learn to show respect and value to someone else while they are speaking.

11. Quit over speaking.

12. Practice and learn to be comfortable with silence.

Change . . . inevitable, unavoidable and waiting for every one of us in some way, shape, or form. Sometimes it comes through different stages and events in our lives. Other times it is of our own making, whether good or bad. But, regardless, it is always a part of the present and future for each of us. The solution is not to avoid change in our lives, but to handle the changes that will be encountered and may become a permanent part of our existence. How can we grow through changes and still remain mentally, emotionally, and spiritually sound? How do we make changes and overcome the fear of losing who we thought we were or who we think we are? How do we become comfortable in situations that may not be of our choosing or desire? Wisdom, discernment, and the attitude we cultivate in handling change in our routine, circumstances, and expectations are a determining factor in the quality of life we live. Whether learned through training, observation, or personal experience, they are a major contributor to a life of less stress, improved health, and better business and personal relationships. They command a higher regard and respect from others.

In our culture and the fast pace of technology, the past is sometimes outdated last week. As change is a part of our society, people, and circumstances, choose a lifestyle and mindset of positive methods toward accepting, implementing and living with change. Use each experience as a "growth hopper," and remember:

Life is full of changes and few things remain stable. Stability does not mean lack of change, but the ability to remain stable in the midst of things changing.

A Biography in Five Short Paragraphs

I walk down the street. There is a deep hole in the sidewalk.
I fall in. I am lost. I am helpless. It isn't my fault.
It takes forever to find a way out.

I walk down the street. There is a deep hole in the sidewalk.
I pretend I don't see it. I fall in. I can't believe I'm in the same place,
but it isn't my fault. It still takes a long time to get out.

I walk down the street. There is a deep hole in the sidewalk.
I see it is there. I still fall in. It is a habit. My eyes are open.
I know where I am. It is my fault. I get out immediately.

I walk down the street. There is a deep hole in the sidewalk.
I walk around it.

I walk down a different street.

— Author unknown

ABOUT
MARYANN MORTON

MaryAnn Morton has a unique and captivating ability to share wisdom, techniques, and direction in a positive, informative, and resourceful manner. Having worked her way from sales through the ranks to an executive management level, she has a vast amount of first hand knowledge to productively relate with the challenges and demands that living one day at a time in a maze of business responsibility, family relationships, personal failures, and successes can bring. In a time when life's pace is fast, feelings are often ignored, and relationships short-lived, it is easy to feel all alone, even in the midst of a crowd. MaryAnn's goal is to touch other lives through proven techniques of supportive and uplifting influence and training. Speaker, musician, author, and 32 year businesswoman, MaryAnn has the ability to take the everyday experiences of life and transform them into a gourmet setting, sprinkled with humor, warmth and insight. You will appreciate and benefit from time spent with MaryAnn.

Contact information:
MaryAnn Morton
Morton Management, Inc.
327 Cahaba River Parc
Birmingham, AL 35243
Phone: (205) 972-8744
Fax: (205) 969-3595
E-mail: MaryAnn@adro.com

FROM FEAR TO FREEDOM IN SIBERIA: CHANGE AS THE DOORWAY TO OPPORTUNITY

by Michael Connor

I. **Unexpected Visitors**

Several years ago, while riding on an overnight train between the cities of Barnaul and Omsk in southern Siberia, I looked out at the sleeping villages and the seemingly endless expanse of snow-covered fields and forests and considered the events of the previous week. Although this was my fifth trip into Siberia to conduct seminars, the past week had been unlike any other, and the twenty-hour train ride and relative peace of my upper berth provided me time to contemplate and process more fully what had recently occurred.

We had just completed a six-day seminar focused on self-awareness, intentional living, and purpose and values clarification with over 100 people in attendance. This was the fourth such seminar conducted in Barnaul, a city of just under a million people not too distant from the Kazakstan border. The previous seminars, while powerful and dynamic within the room itself, had not drawn the type of attention as the one just completed.

On the second day of the training we were visited by representatives from the Russian administrative police, military police, and FSB (formerly the KGB) — six police and/or secret service personnel in total. I temporarily entrusted the people in the room to a Russian colleague, and met, with the assistance of a translator, with our "guests" outside the room. Due to what I later discovered was a reaction by territorial psycho-therapists and an FSB mandate to track "non-traditional" seminar and educational programs, our seminar was now viewed as illegal, and I was to appear in Russian court the following morning.

I began to consider one of the principles foundational to the seminars I lead: *use everything to learn, uplift, and grow.* "Everything" is self-explanatory. The good, bad, ugly, beautiful, and unexpected — whatever shows up. What was presenting itself this seminar was a date in Russian court, a scenario with which I had no prior experience and no clear sense, at least initially, of what the possible outcomes might be. Questions raced through my mind as I committed, once again, to put into practice the principles I had been sharing with thousands of people on four continents. How was I going to transform this challenge into an opportunity? How could I most effectively shift from fear into effective focus and action when, while images of the Gulag danced in my head, I felt at the mercy of a culture and system so different from my own? How could I provide a model for all those involved while also ensuring my own safety? I pondered these thoughts and others throughout that evening and into the following morning.

II. A World in Flux

What do we mean when we say that we live in a world of change? Intellectually we know that each moment differs, if even slightly, from both the one preceding and following it. No two moments can be exactly alike. Time passes, our bodies age, and our minds process new bits of information. Considered globally, it becomes even more apparent, as within any given moment there are births, deaths, ideas born, and decisions initiated. This is as it's always been, and yet, somehow, this change seems much more apparent to us now. Information essential for making effective business decisions is dated almost as soon as it reaches us, assumptions more often than not lead to costly miscalculations and oversights, and projections and extrapolations must be updated so frequently that it sometimes seems counterproductive to develop them in the first place.

Our intense desire to feel in control of our future and to plan with a high level of certainty is being challenged. We can no longer assume that the foundational thinking, institutionalized beliefs, and established practices of today will apply tomorrow. This can be terrifying to those powerful and more primitive aspects of ourselves and our brains that are most geared towards survival and that crave to control what is ahead in hopes of ensuring the safety of our future and reducing the risk associated with the unknown.

When faced with this uncertainty, and when not guided by our more developed human aspects, we will tend towards the fight, flight, or freeze response, all the result of fear. When we look around us, we see the result of fear and its impact at home, at work, and in the world where we live. We need a way to transform this fear into a more effective emotional and intellectual response to support us in thriving, rather than floundering, in the midst of change. We need a new set of tools that are designed for and tailored to a world that seems constantly in flux.

"Trouble is only opportunity in work clothes."
— Henry J. Kaiser

III. Holding On and Letting Go

While the events in Barnaul were unique, they differed little from the multitude of situations that present themselves in our lives, whether at work or at home, in that what we assumed would happen did not. We, the local seminar organizers and myself, were faced with the unexpected and the range of emotions associated with unanticipated and, as it seemed in the moment, unwanted change. We decided to apply the three basic principles that are the foundation for thriving on change:

1. Understand what to hold to and what to let go of.
2. Be willing to let go.
3. Focus on the opportunities, rather than the fear, when facing the unknown or the unpredictable.

Understanding what to hold on to and what to let go of requires a present time inventory and assessment of the situation that answers the questions, "What is so now?" and "Where do we want to go from here?" in that order. If we do not honestly assess the situation as it currently stands, we run the risk of maintaining an attachment to and acting out of assumptions made prior to the changes. Conducting an honest inventory can often be challenging due to the fact that we tend to get attached to our ideas, beliefs, and plans. We are driven by a strong and very basic need to be "right" about our beliefs and assumptions that filter and distort our ability to conduct a neutral, impartial, and fully honest evaluation of the situation. Our ability to take effective inventory will directly impact our ability to effectively establish a new set of clear goals and desired outcomes. It can be valuable, and is often essential, to bring in someone from outside the situation to assist with this assessment process, be it a friend, colleague, or professional facilitator or consultant.

The process of holding on and letting go often challenges us to look at what is most essential or the primary purpose for any given undertaking. Personal agendas, ego attachments, and the seemingly ever-present posturing and positioning for control must all be rooted up and out. Questions such as "Why are we doing this?" and "What do we really want?" often assist us in identifying what is truly most important, if we're willing to go past the initial, superficial answers and into the deeper and/or higher motivations for our undertakings. Change demands each of us to focus on what is vital and to eliminate all of the extraneous distractions. When we are able to access the truest purpose for our actions, not only is there greater clarity regarding what to hold on to and what to let go of, but we also find letting go to be easier and more natural in the light of this clearer understanding of what matters most.

Connecting to our truest purpose allows us to begin to see the opportunities in the present situation, even if it varies greatly from what we had intended in the first place. As we let go of our attachments and clarify our purpose, we may even begin to see greater opportunities for expressing that purpose than existed before. Unanticipated change can remove the tunnel vision that often comes with the attachment to one specific outcome and open the doorway to numerous other, sometimes more advantageous, scenarios. As we begin to focus on these opportunities, rather than on the fear, the natural result is enthusiasm and creativity. We fill the unknown with creative possibilities for manifesting the purpose that drove our efforts in the first place.

IV. A Newly Formed Team Finds a Common Purpose

Following my meeting with our police and secret service friends, I returned to the seminar room and updated the participants on the situation. I wasn't sure how they'd react, but I knew that the only way to begin an effective assessment of the situation was to acknowledge what was currently happening. My willingness to share openly with the group, rather than conceal what had occurred outside the room, resulted in a rallying of support, out of which came a lawyer willing to assist us with the legal process. That evening and the following morning the local organizers of the seminar, the lawyer, and I met to evaluate the situation and clarify how we could transform this obstacle into an opportunity.

We assessed the situation, deferring greatly to those in the group, especially our legal counsel, who had experience with the local authorities and legal system. While I was the one in charge inside the room and ultimately responsible for the seminar, I needed to surrender a large chunk of that role to others as we took inventory and clarified a new set of desirable outcomes. When change occurs, one of the assumptions that we must sometimes reconsider is whether those chosen to execute a plan or empowered to produce an outcome are still the most suited to do so. New information and experience may be required, and new members may need to be added to the team while others may need to step away or change roles. Expect personal agendas and ego attachment to kick in during this process, as mine did in Barnaul.

I found myself struggling between wanting to be in control, surrendering completely to whatever the others decided, and being a contributing member of the new, not yet clearly defined, team. One of the first things for me to let go of was my pattern of either being in charge or relinquishing responsibility completely. The decisions we made as a group were going to affect me directly, and yet I was not qualified to take the lead in the discussion. I continued in a somewhat confused state regarding my place on the new team until we, as a group, were able to clarify our purpose for being together. What had originally brought us all together in Barnaul was a seminar, individually and as a group we needed to dig deeper and answer two critical questions: "Why are we doing this?" and "What do we really want?" We generated a common purpose, based on the very principles in the seminar we were conducting, including focusing on a win/win solution, communicating openly and honestly, and developing an empathy and understanding for other points of view. Also, following our assessment of the situation, we clarified and agreed upon a series of desired outcomes regarding the seminar and the short and long- term safety of all involved. We built our new team based on these commonly shared values and agreed upon outcomes. I stepped into the role of facilitator and supported the process by both testing and challenging the assumptions of the team and keeping us on track regarding our stated outcomes.

V. Determining What's Non-Negotiable

Every effectively lived life or effectively run team or organization has, at its core, a succinct purpose and a set of foundational values. Sometimes these are clearly stated; other times they are simply expressed through the actions and activities of the individuals or leaders involved. Purpose and values are not to be confused with goals and vision, which tend to be time-specific and more quantifiable. While goals change, core purpose and values do not. Core purpose and values are not, or should not be, negotiable.

When we don't take the time to clarify our truest purpose, we often confuse intention and method. This confusion creates attachment to the specific goals or outcomes being sought. We don't know what to hold to, what is not negotiable, and so, in our insecurity, we try to hold on to everything, for fear of losing it all. This attachment makes change an enemy and the process of change painful, leading to ineffectiveness in times of transition.

To truly thrive in the midst of change, we must first know what will not change. We must differentiate what the intention is and what the methods are towards that intention. Knowing what to hold on to gives us the security to let go of everything else, if necessary. The fear associated with letting go is lessened when we realize that even greater opportunities for fulfilling our stated purpose are at hand. Our truest purpose and values provide the compass that guides each of us and our teams and organizations during times of change.

> *"Perfection of means and confusion of goals seem,*
> *in my opinion, to characterize our age."*
>
> — Albert Einstein

VI. A Day in Court

Early March is still the heart of winter in Siberia. After planning and preparing our legal defense, we drove over the icy streets of Barnaul to the police headquarters and courthouse on the other side of the city. I had no idea what to expect once we arrived, so I simply focused on our purpose and goals.

There are times when surrendering intellectual control over to intuitive or divine guidance is simply the most effective choice available. This frigid Friday morning was one of those times. Upon arrival, we waited in a crowded hallway before being ushered into the courtroom.

Awaiting us were the FSB agents and military police we'd met with the night before. Our case was presented before one judge, who would determine its outcome. It soon became clear that the charges were being directed both at me, the presenter and facilitator of the seminar, as well as towards the local organizing body, and the FSB agents and police intended to state their case strongly. I wondered what unseen forces were motivating their actions, but I would only begin to fully understand as this drama unfolded. I mostly observed and listened, focusing on understanding their point of view, ensuring our points were communicated effectively without animosity, and focusing on a win/win solution. In my own brief statements, I was able to communicate, through my translator, much the same, acknowledging that they had a job to do and offering to explore possibilities that allowed them to do their job while permitting us to complete our seminar and effectively conduct future seminars in the city.

I was relieved when the judge acquitted me and was impressed with his neutrality in weighing the facts involved prior to coming to a decision. I was, however, disappointed when he chose in favor of the police in relation to the local organizers and the seminar itself. This meant that to continue the seminar would place those people responsible locally at risk with the authorities. Once again, we were thrown into change, and, once again, we needed to assess the situation, clarify our purpose, and revisit our desired outcomes.

VII. An Ongoing Process

Many of us have been taught to approach change like a bad dream — just get through it and return to the safety of the known. This approach may have worked, to some degree, when the pace of life was slower and events were more predictable. As change continues to accelerate, however, we begin to find ourselves in what feels like a never-ending transition. Change is no longer the anomaly, but the norm, and a new outlook and paradigm for working with change are required. We might refer to such an approach as "anticipating the unexpected." How do we live and work most effectively in a world where we are frequently confronted with the unexpected, about which we may know very little or nothing at all? While there are no easy answers to this question, the following guidelines can assist individuals, teams, and organizations prepare for the unexpected:

1. Clarify and maintain focus on your truest purpose or intention, and allow the methods to be flexible.

2. Build teams and organizations that are diverse in terms of skill

sets, personalities, and competencies, but consistent in terms of purpose and values.

3. Create all goals and plans knowing they will change — for the better — along the way, when the underlying purpose is running the process.

4. Learn how to develop, utilize, and act on your intuition.

5. Develop the ability to be confident without having to be "right." Be willing "not to know" — because you don't, no matter how much experience or information you have at your disposal.

6. Remember that, although change seems to happen suddenly, you participate in its creation. There are always indicators or red flags that, when you are paying attention, let you know what lies ahead.

The acceleration of change brings us face to face with the dichotomies of life and with the need to find a way to bring these seemingly opposing qualities together within us and within our teams. To thrive in the midst of change, we must be both unwavering and flexible, confident and humble, intelligent and intuitive, leading and following. Most of all we must learn to trust ourselves enough to let go the past and be willing to live and make decisions in the present. When we are living in the present, not only are we more effective at dealing with change when it occurs, but we are more effective at recognizing the often intuitive indicators that let us know what is ahead. That information allows us not only to prepare for such events, but also to redirect ourselves, when appropriate, towards more preferable outcomes.

VIII. Courage and Victory in Barnaul

As our lawyer friend tried to uncover the legal basis for the judge's decision and understand the driving force behind the investigation, our local organizers had a decision to make. They had spent over six months organizing and promoting the seminar, with people attending from the Barnaul region and beyond. While they had put their time, money, and hearts into this event, continuing the seminar could result in fines, loss of professional licenses, or worse. I could simply facilitate and support their process of choosing, letting go of any attachment or personal agenda I had to completing the seminar. The stakes, for those who might potentially be impacted, were simply too high.

What I observed next was an extraordinary demonstration of courage and commitment. The organizers, including two in particular who were most at risk, chose to continue the seminar. Their decision came as a result of one of their core values and their primary motivation for organizing the seminar in the first place — freedom. The freedom to choose how they lived their lives, the freedom to voice their opinion, the freedom to stand up for what they believed in. They chose to stand for what they held true.

We continued the seminar later that day and once again were visited by the FSB agents. This time they took one of the local organizers to the police station for questioning. In the face of intensive questioning, she stood her ground, communicating through her actions and words her truest purpose and values. She was released only after being served a summons to appear in court the following morning. She returned to the seminar room shortly after we concluded the evening's activities and updated the rest of us, including the lawyer. She was advised by the lawyer to find some way to postpone the court date until after the seminar, allowing the seminar to conclude before a verdict was reached. With courage and commitment comes creativity. She contacted a physician friend, who had her admitted to a local hospital for the weekend with "bronchitis." Clearly, wherever there is a system designed to control or contain the human spirit, that same spirit finds ways around it. She would not be able to appear in court due to a medical condition.

While we hoped that this latest maneuver would throw the FSB off our scent for the weekend, we were mistaken. The next day the agents actually entered the room while I was leading the group in an exercise. As I saw them enter, I feared that we had played all our cards and they would now stop the seminar, disband the group, and haul the organizers off to jail. To my amazement, the participants began yelling comments and insults towards the agents regarding the breach of their democratic rights and freedom of choice. Although I was tempted to join them, I asked them to stop, reminding them to focus on a win/win solution and noting that the agents were simply doing their job. I sent the participants on a break, so the organizers and the agents could discuss the situation. At the back of the room, while waiting for an update, I noticed that while my thoughts were clear and focused, my body was shaking. I could hide my fears from my mind, but not my body. I recommitted to focus on my highest purpose, and what had brought me to Siberia in the first place. What transpired next was quite extraordinary.

The agents, unable to get one of the two people legally responsible for the seminar into court, had come for the other. She was not, however, at the seminar, several of the other organizers explained to the agents, but somewhere else in the city, possibly at her home. One of the other organizers offered to "assist" the agents by riding with them to her home and other locations they might likely find her, all the while quite aware that the woman they were seeking was hiding behind the stage inside the room itself. We later found out that as this organizer drove around the city with the agents she shared with great passion why this seminar was so important to her and the others involved. The agents, well aware they were being taken on a wild goose chase and persuaded by the resoluteness of their navigator, finally agreed to receiving a signature on a document they needed to return to their superiors verifying a court date the following week.

> *"You can cage the singer but not the song."*
> — Henry Belafonte

Inside the room I was aware that the agents were being escorted around the city, but it wasn't at all clear they wouldn't be back. I decided to continue the seminar but wanted to somehow calm down the participants. Given that we utilize music at points throughout the seminar, I asked our music coordinator, a Russian with very little English fluency, to find a song that might soothe the tense, anxious energy that was present. As people entered the room, he chose, to my astonishment, "Let It Be" by the Beatles. As the words, ". . . and when the night is cloudy there is still a light that shines on me . . ." played, I stepped behind a curtain and wept, all the emotion flooding out of me. The fear, the courage, the freedom, the love. What an opportunity this had been for me and so many others to access the truth within and allow it to guide us through the darkness of the unknown.

The seminar concluded without further incident and was one of the most powerful and positive that I've ever experienced. The challenges and changes had assisted us all in clarifying what was really important — freedom, truth, and courage. While several of the local organizers did appear in court the following week, the fines they incurred were minimal. Information generated by our lawyer friend has assisted local organizers in developing a plan that will allow for a win/win approach with local authorities. We continue to do seminars in Siberia, where the challenges and changes continue, providing, in each case, a new doorway to opportunity.

ABOUT
MICHAEL CONNOR

*M*ichael Connor is the President of Creative Transitions: Transforming Challenges into Opportunities, a company specializing in assisting organizations, teams, and individuals in thriving, excelling, and profiting in the midst of change. He has designed and presented keynotes and seminars worldwide since 1993. He is the former President and CEO of the Insight Educational Institute and a lead facilitator for Insight Seminars Worldwide. A former health care executive with a wealth of business and management expertise, Mike has presented on four continents, and holds Masters Degrees in Health Care Management and Practical Theology. While consulting to the Ministry of Health in Bulgaria, he met his wife, Maria, a physician. They and their two children reside near Boston.

Contact information:
Michael Connor
Creative Transitions
8 Nauset Road
Brockton, MA 02301
Phone: (508) 584-9062
Fax: (508) 580-6466
E-mail: MC@ThriveOnChange.com
Website: www.ThriveOnChange.com

WHAT MAKES A THRIVER?

by Liz Taylor, Ph.D.

At the end of my day as a counselor I am always in awe of my client's life stories. Why do some clients thrive in transition and others fall apart? Is it genetic, a skill, or pure luck?

Transitions are changes, a process or instance of changing from one state, activity or place to another. As a psychologist, I am fascinated by individuals' "resilience," the ability of a person to spring back with strength and spirit quickly. I wish I could buy it in tablet form, but I can't; I can only assist clients in developing it. Resilience, tenacity, and vision are important traits to develop to succeed in life. Most clients see their life in two dimensions, personal (relationships) and business (career). It is the balancing and harmony of these that creates a successful life. The following are two cases that illustrate that when your world falls apart, how your resilience, tenacity, and commitment to your vision can energize you into a thriver!

Meet Ms. Energy. At 45 years old she had it all: a husband, two children, and a beautiful home. She had an exciting career, plus a stock portfolio, making them part of the new millionaire generation. However, she was not happy. Why not, I wondered. What more could she want?

It turned out that Ms. Energy was the youngest of four children and had learned at a very young age how to please people. She was so good at it she lost herself. For 25 years she was married to a self-absorbed man who thought of her as a trophy. He did not respect her and neither did her teenagers, but she was always there for them, "dancing" (doing everything possible to keep everyone happy and on an even keel). She was quite a master, and all her friends thought she had a perfect marriage. But she felt very empty, guilty about feeling this way, and afraid to tell anyone. For more than two years she stayed in a cloud of depression, alone and silent.

One cold, November day, her world came crashing down and she could no longer dance. She entered my office, saying, "My life is perfect, but I am hurting, what is wrong with me?" Through counseling, Ms. Energy learned that she did not ask for help or put limits on her relationships. She believed by over-loving her family members they would see their selfish ways. No such luck! As she became more self-aware of her needs and asked for assistance, her family became upset. Her husband told her sons, "It's hormones, lookout!" But it was a woman's cry for help!

Her poem said she thought she should move away from everyone. I pointed out to her that escaping was not the answer because her pattern of caretaking, or enabling, would still be there until she changed. She was very angry, and stated, "Doctor Liz, you keep wanting to know how I feel, well here it is." She handed me a poem, "My Comfort Zone" which really says it all. Tears flowed down her cheeks as she finally spoke the truth. She admitted that couple counseling was a joke to her husband. They had grown apart, he was not trustworthy, and was verbally abusive. "Why do you want to stay," I asked.

"Because I *love* him and can't make it without him," she sobbed. Really? It sounds to me, like you've been doing everything by yourself for a long time anyway and succeeding." I set my yellow writing pad down and stated, "You! Ms. Energy are resourceful, capable, and have many choices."

"I do," she responded softly.

"Yes! and now is the time to get out of your comfort zone and reclaim yourself."

My Comfort Zone

I used to have my "Comfort Zone," where I knew I couldn't fail.
The same four walls of busy work, were really more like a jail.
I longed so much to do the things that I'd never done before.
But I stayed inside my "Comfort Zone," pacing the same old floor.
I said it didn't matter, that I wasn't doing much.
I said I didn't care for things like diamonds, furs and such.
I claimed to be so busy, with the things inside my zone.
But deep inside I longed for something special of my own.

I couldn't let my life go by, just watching others win.
I held my breath and stepped outside to let the change begin.
I took a step and with new strength, I've never felt before . . .
*I kissed my "Comfort Zone," **"Good-bye!"***
and closed and locked the door.

If you are in a "Comfort Zone," and afraid to venture out,
just remember that all winners were at one time filled with doubt.
A step or two forward with a few words of encouragement
and praise to others can make dreams come true.
Greet your future with courage and a smile . . .
Success is there for you!

*Disclaimer: Ms. Energy's poem was adapted from several poems.

Let's begin by looking at your strengths and answering the following five questions.

1. What are your talents or skills that have made you succeed in the past? (Organized, able to multitask, friendly, cooperative, a great negotiator)

2. What would you really enjoy doing? What are you passionate about?

3. List your bad habits that have stopped you from succeeding in the past. (Always late, no time management skills, careless about returning phone calls)

4. What word phrases do you hear in your mind from childhood that haunt you? ("You'll never make it, you are too lazy to succeed, you are stupid.")

5. Create your vision by detailing the life you want, write it out in detail on paper what you will be doing, with whom and where. Today, begin believing it is possible and it is happening.

Ms. Energy learned through this process that she had many skills, and her vision was to take her company from a home business to a national level. She developed a plan with the following four steps to:

1. Increase her knowledge of financing and taxes for her business by utilizing the IRS's free training programs and attending the local small business association's meetings.

2. Update her counseling skills by completing a graduate degree from a local college. Interestingly, she did not tell anyone of her plans because her voices of the past haunted her. She wanted to prove to herself that she could do it. Besides, her family members were all self-absorbed.

3. Start her dream by taking one small step at a time. She began by creating a flyer on her seminar company, *Soaring into Success*, offering luncheon seminars to businesses. She was a hit! Soon, she began presenting three- to six-hour training seminars.

4. Develop a support network by hiring consultants with a different area of expertise from hers and create a winning team. Together they have even won local awards.

Although Ms. Energy encountered many roadblocks on her journey to success, they were just temporary because her life philosophy was "problems are opportunities for growth!" She was recently quoted in a newspaper article as saying, "Job and relationships do end, signaling it's time to soar like an eagle out of your comfort zone and live your dream/vision."

Ms. Energy's story demonstrates that resilience is an essential skill in surviving. In addition, it demonstrates how transitional periods are teaching times, and that creating a plan of action that includes "baby steps," allows an individual to soar into success.

Story 2: Ms. M.

Have you ever been getting dressed for work and sat on the bed and asked, "Do I really want to work today, and/or is this all there is?" Meet Ms. M., a 55 year-old sales executive with 33 years in the same company. Everyone around her said, "Relax you can retire soon!" "Retire," she mused, "I want more. If I am going to work this hard it will be for my dream!"

In late September, she entered my office, requesting assistance from an executive coach. As a certified coach, at the first meeting, it's important to get on the same page as the client, to understand his or her perceptions and motivations for change. I do this by asking the following questions:

1. Why now?

For Ms. M., she had been in a relationship for five years and had realized the man she loved did not know how to spell COMMITMENT, let alone practice it.

2. What is your vision or dream? Describe it in detail.

I explained to Ms. M that *"your vision is only clear when you can look into your heart"* (a favorite Carl Jung saying of mine). She had great insight and knew what she wanted. She desired to return to Sacramento, where her family lived, and to assist her sister by marketing her company and transforming it from a regional position to a national level. The key here is that her vision was clear and concise.

3. Map out your progress: step by step . . .

What steps are required to move from now to your vision?

4. Put your plan in motion.

Remember the goal is progress not perfection; it's ok to modify and redefine the steps.

5. Create a support network, utilizing your resources.

The following pages detail Ms. M.'s progress as she put her plan into motion. She thought the opportunity was right and talked to family and friends. They all agreed that a change would be good. She hired a coach to help her make decision-making and avoid common errors.

Step 1: Sell my Home.

Hire a realtor with a proven marketing and sales record.

Step 2: Sold the House.

It only took two months to sell the house. I was so excited the first step of my dream was becoming a reality. The price was right, there was only one problem, a contingency. Yes, you guessed it, the sale fell through. Back to Step ONE.

Step 1: Re-list House.

Coaching guidance: Make sure to hold an open house for agents from all over town and offer a bonus for a quick sale!

Step 2: I Sold my House.

The house sold within one week this time. I had a new buyer, no contingency, their credit was good, and the house closed in 30 days. I gave my notice again and the celebration was on.

Step 3: Leaving and Saying Goodbye.

Shopping for a moving company was an experience. Once the bids were in I made my selection. The other moving companies kept calling to assure me that they had a better offer, and they wanted me to fax them the winner's bid so they could match it. I finally turned off the telephone. The moving van representative delivered boxes and tape. I forgot that I would have to pack. Not an easy task, considering I had lived in this house for nine years. My wonderful friends were there for me. I don't know how I would have done it without them. They kept me focused, which left no time for memories. There were only a few tense times and now I can laugh about those.

Coaching guidance: Ms. M. gave her exit interview to her boss. He was very excited for her but a little envious that he wasn't making a career change. She made a very smart move by asking for a leave of absence for three months. This protected her from the chance that a transfer from the Sacramento branch might not happen. She had learned from selling her house, the number one rule about transitions. That is, to plan for Murphy's Law, "what ever can happen, will happen," so be prepared. In addition, she had developed the gift of humor, which is key to succeeding in transitions. When you can laugh at the situation and yourself, you are on the road to healing.

Step 4: Moving to California.

I packed my car, put my little pug, Pookie, in the front seat with me, and said good bye to my friends with tears in my eyes for the times we had shared, the memories I had of my beautiful home, and the love I had lost. Putting the tears away for another day, I began smiling, singing as I clocked the miles to sunny California. Being a Christian and an optimist, I knew that God had a plan for me, but at that moment I was at a loss as to what that might be. All I did know was that I was on the highway to a new life.

Coaching guidance: Ms. M. was easy to work with and coach through this transition because her vision was well defined. Plus, she believed in herself and knew that to advance, she had to take a risk. We had calculated her risk, meaning she had taken stock of her life and added up the positive reasons to stay in her job versus the reasons to take a chance. In addition, Ms. M. was willing to take a lesser paying job because money wasn't her motivator; it was her family and finding self-fulfillment. And guess what? Her new home and new job gave her a 30 percent salary increase. Do you want to know the details of how she succeeded? Log on to Feel Good Seminars.com and identify yourself as a Thriver.

Remember, in times of transition a sounding board, an executive coach, or a psychologist can assist you in defining your path and avoiding some common dead ends. Follow the 4 P's a day rule: pray, plan, proceed, and pursue persistently. Make an effort to talk to others who have survived transitional periods and read. Three favorite books that I recommend are: *The Bible, Feel The Fear and Do It Anyway,* by Susan Jeffers and *9 Steps to Financial Freedom* by Suze Orman.

The roads of adventure and success are yours to enjoy if you remember to plan and take the steps one at a time. Learning to laugh during the road blocks will help turn your stress into fuel that will energize you through the journey.

Life is too short, so decide today to step out of your comfort zone, and live your dream. Let Ms. M.'s words, "change is not only good for you, it looks good on you!" motivate you to venture out.

ABOUT
LIZ TAYLOR, PH.D.

*D*r. Elizabeth Taylor is a clinical psychologist completing her Post-Doctoral work in California. She is also a certified executive coach. She speaks throughout the United States on Transitions, the Beginning Adventure for Living Your Dream. She is president, of Feel Good Seminars, in Lincoln California. She appears on television, provides radio talk hosts with answers, and last but not least, co-authored the best seller, Living Light and Healthy, with over 350,000 copies sold. She graduated with a degree in Nutritional Science from Arizona State University and has worked for twenty years as a registered dietitian, empowering clients to live a healthy life by balancing their diet and exercise while minding their moods. She has been a college professor for 18 years, lecturing on the topics of child and family development, and exercise and nutrition at American River College and Sierra College. "Teaching is my passion," she states. "Sharing my expertise has enriched my life and has given me the energy to succeed."

Contact information:
Liz Taylor, Ph.D.
Feel Good Seminars
2575 First Street
Lincoln, CA 95648
Phone: (916) 434-9460
E-mail: LizTaylorrd@Yahoo.com
Website: www.Feel-Good-Seminars.com

SHIFTING WORKPLACE COMPETENCIES: THREE PRACTICES THAT EMBRACE CHANGE

by Cheryl Moser, Ph.D.

Career-Minded Professionals Wanted: Assist a rapidly growing company to take a leadership role in today's ever-changing marketplace. Management seeking to add a flexible team member who is an innovative problem-solver and can readily manage change. Competencies required: Ability to build strong working relationships with others, welcome the use of technology in the work-place, practice highly effective communication skills, and utilize good judgment when making decisions. Seeking a lifelong learner who can get up-to-speed quickly. Only those who believe their qualifications are a good fit with our company need apply.

Often, today's job requirements reflect the ideas found in this employment ad. Would you apply? Notice the ad is not seeking, as we see on reality television mean-spirited, devious, scheming, manipulative tribe members. To the contrary, it is searching for winning individuals who thrive when working within a transformational organization. Clearly, the individuals considered for these positions will be team players with impressive interpersonal competencies. Today, it is not wise at work to be heard humming Frank Sinatra's famous song *I Did It My Way*.

Since the recent turn-of-the-century, organizations have been forced to make transformational changes to adapt to the continuous changes in our world's increasingly competitive marketplace. Presently, change in the workplace is the driving force behind many new feelings of today's employees. I recently overheard my friend Ryan droning on to his colleague Anne, "The only thing we seem to be able to count on anymore in this place is that things will change." I believe Anne's apathetic grunt acknowledged her agreement. Even though we all feel less secure with the many transitions in our lives today, I say forcefully, "Not to fear! Everything in the new world of work has not changed." When I was a little girl my Yodda-like Girl Scout leader taught me the motto, "Be Prepared." That basic principle holds true today and may still serve us well as a survival skill to meet new challenges at work.

Prepare for this new world of work by changing several of your current practices in the workplace. Some people, who profess to liking themselves just fine the way they are, may ask, "Does this mean I have to give up myself to be appreciated by the company?" No! Today, "being prepared," means learning to accept, support, adapt, and even welcome change in new roles and in new role expectations. Becoming an employee who thrives in the midst of change may or may not include compensation of a million dollars in the near future; however, it may mean waking up in the morning and looking forward to going to work. Furthermore, by adapting to the recent shift in desirable workplace competencies, you will increase your worth to a company. Begin expanding your expertise by learning more about three workplace practices that embrace change:

— Welcome Technology as a Tool in the Workplace
— Focus on Building Strong Working Relationships
— Demonstrate Effective Interpersonal Communication Skills

Welcoming Technology as a Tool in the Workplace

Not in his goals but in his
Transitions man is great.

— Ralph Waldo Emerson

My recently retired minister used to playfully say, "If you want to make God laugh, tell him your plans." I believe Pastor Ward's humor was not discouraging me from making plans but instead was encouraging my preparedness for change. One area of workplace change that most of us can identify with is the increasing use of computers. With new technological information, this area of change seems to be occurring at an accelerated speed. No use trying to hide from change; instead, accept it and adjust to it. Years ago, I tried hiding from difficult changes at work. I soon found out that I was not any better at the game of hide and seek as an adult at work than I was as a kid playing in my neighborhood at dusk.

At work, just like back in the neighborhood, I somehow manage to become the target of heat-seeking missile type people who easily find me and force me out of hiding. I did "come out, come out, from wherever you are" and enhanced my computer skills in order to meet the company's new demands. I confess that I am proud of myself for taking on this new challenge. Proud that I did not panic and overreact by being irrational and thinking I had to become a "techno wizard," I understood that I merely needed to start by expanding my comfort zone with computers. Finally, I must also confess, "own up and come clean" as my kids would say, to the lessons learned from this and similar transitional experiences. I would describe the transitional process as coming to terms with my new situation as a result of organizational change. These lessons were learned as I began fine-tuning several of my competencies to better fit the needs of today's workplace.

Transition Lesson #1: Staying informed and having an open attitude towards change is important because I now realize that new technologies I once believed extraneous have turned out to be today's essentials.

Transition Lesson #2: The transitional process of moving from denial, to high anxiety, to anger, to acceptance, to creativity, to enthusiasm was not a linear path for me. Once I had the courage to go through the process and not try to go around it, I experienced increased self-esteem. We often feel our best when achieving goals that are particularly the most personally challenging for us.

Transition Lesson #3: Learning to tolerate the early uncomfortable feelings of ambiguity and uncertainty that accompany change significantly contributed to the fact that I was later able to become even more laser focused on achieving my goals.

Transition Lesson #4: I noticed that the company was aware of the fact that several of us have demonstrated that we are lifelong learners by proactively improving targeted workplace practices. More importantly, I noticed that the company realizes crabby, set-in-his-ways Charlie is not going to take the initiative to improve his competencies. They further realize that even sending him off for an intense week's training in Emotional Stability 101 would not help. Charlie could not quickly change the fact that he cannot handle stress well, has a negative view of the future, avoids conflict to a fault, and never seems to be able to recover from setbacks and disappointments in the workplace.

Transition Lesson #5: I no longer cringe when my boss approaches me with that famous opening sentence of his, "Cheryl, glad I found you. I want to discuss a great opportunity for you that has just come up." Looking back on those moments and as to why I would wince and grimace in response to his cheerfulness, I found a simple answer. I always knew it to be true that I liked new learning, considered myself innovative, and certainly preferred variety and challenge to performing routine, uninteresting tasks at work. It was simply my feelings of fear and uncertainty that were causing my reluctance. I have worked on replacing those feelings with a more courageous attitude and the willingness to take risks. Will Rogers' words inspired me as I remembered his saying, "Why not go out on a limb? That's where the fruit is."

Transition Lesson #6: I personally learned firsthand that someone who cannot learn how to turn the blinking light off her VCR can still quickly figure out to use computers as an effective tool at work. Utilizing the right equipment gives us the advantage over the competition. I learned to adopt a welcoming attitude towards the latest equipment and advances in technology.

Transition Lesson #7: I now appreciate the words of the French novelist André Gide who wrote, "One does not discover new lands without consenting to lose sight of the shore for a very long time." The further I moved away from my old ways, the more I felt the excitement, intrinsic motivation, and refocused energies that come with new beginnings.

Focus on Building Strong Working Relationships

Be a team player, not because it diffuses blame, but because it adds value to your effectiveness at work. Companies have need of employees who are both highly effective team players, as well as useful individual contributors.

Hearing the views of others seems to validate my own research findings. Alyson, my colleague who has been an effective manager for the last fifteen years, claims, "Today, managers are seeking team players that can leave their ego at the door when entering important decision-making meetings." My friend Sam, who started his own successful business ten years ago, learned that the biggest worry he and other business owners have today is that, "When it comes to putting forth the energy it takes to function as part of a self-empowered work team, we find some of our employees seem to have recently retired while still on the payroll." This is good news to hear for those of us who are not ego-maniacs suffering from workplace burnout. With the current need for team players and good team leadership, we must take the initiative to honestly look at and possibly improve our potential for building future relationships at work.

It is common to hear words and phrases in today's workplace like: collaborative efforts, participatory management, customer-driven planning, temporary special assignments, cross-functional teams, implementing new technology, change management, leading strategic hiring teams, and, needless to say, mergers and acquisitions. A common denominator to all these activities is that we must work well with others.

Before you begin the process of strengthening your ability to build strong working relationships, partnerships, and alliances, you may want to mull over your answers to the following questions:

1. Over a period of time, what reputation has my behavior earned me at work?
2. How well do I get along with my current boss?
3. Do I make connections with people through sharing common goals, concerns, and outcomes?
4. Do I have a basic understanding of the group process and of the common behavior of team members?
5. As a team member, do I welcome a group culture where the sharing of diverse opinions and ideas is encouraged while working with others to find common ground?
6. Am I not only valuable to the company, but to other employees?
7. Am I perceived as cooperative toward my employees, colleagues, and management?

The field of social science often provides us with relevant information regarding influences on group behavior. Raising our level of understanding may help us proactively prevent group or member behavior that inhibits team problem solving, results in poor decision-making, and undermines group cohesiveness. We have often seen this behavior before, but now it has a name to it.

Groupthink is a group decision-making style characterized by excessive concurrence among group members. When this occurs, the group loses its perspective. Groups need to make sure that their need for agreement is not stronger than their motivation to gather accurate knowledge and make good decisions.

Social Loafing is reflected in the reduction of an individual's output on easy tasks when group members' contributions are pooled. This behavior poses a threat to group productivity. Social loafing can be reduced when workers believe their individual contributions are identifiable.

Prosocial Behavior refers to any act performed with the goal of benefiting another person. This often requires empathy: the ability to put oneself in the shoes of another person.

Sources of Conflict in the workplace often falls into two major categories: interpersonal and organizational. Studies show that the majority of conflicts are interpersonally based. *Interpersonal Conflict:* Occurs when an individual perceives or values a situation differently from the way another in the workplace perceives or values the same situation. *Organizational Conflict:* Occurs often as a by-product of change within the organization. In addition to change, sources of organizational conflict may be from limited resources, conflicting goals and objectives, and poor planning or communication.

Group Polarization is the exaggeration through group discussions of the initial tendencies in the thinking of group members. This is more likely to occur on important issues than on those considered trivial. Having diverse team members reduces this effect.

Good Mood Effect refers to the fact that a good mood increases helping behavior. In turn, helping behavior increases good feelings and positive thoughts.

Process Loss is any aspect of group interaction that inhibits good problem solving. Reasons for this effect include not listening well to those of low status, allowing some members to dominate while others tune out, and the group's unwillingness to put forth the needed effort to find out who are the most competent members of the group on this particular issue.

Failure to Share Unique Information refers to members' failure to share pertinent information that only they know with the rest of the group. No one member is an expert on all aspects of a current problem. A sense of trust and collaboration is needed for members to share their particular expertise with the rest of the group. Yet, to reach the best decision, the group must pool their resources.

Workplace Stress refers to the negative feelings and beliefs that people have when they think they cannot cope with the current demands from their environment. The coping style an individual uses to deal with stress depends on personality type and what has successfully worked in the past.

Production Blocking is an artifact of group discussion by which the number of ideas any given member generates is limited by the member's capacity to remember what he or she was going to say while listening closely to another talking. This may often reduce the number of ideas generated during brainstorming sessions. Breaking into smaller groups may be a solution.

Group Decisions are often more extreme in position and riskier than individual outcomes, in part because groups diffuse responsibilities. These group decisions are highly productive when all group members are extremely knowledgeable as a result of shared information.

Know Your Strengths

While on vacation your backpacking group gets lost in the wilderness; let's hope the team has diverse backgrounds and a collection of useful traits and skills. Diversity of members will significantly improve their team problem solving ability. One member with knowledge of hypothermia may be as valuable as another member who can quickly spot a shelter utilizing the immediate environment at hand. Still other people may be adept at signaling rescue efforts or possess the skills needed to keep the group calm and focused. Who knows, a detailed-oriented person who is highly observant may prove the most valuable member by spotting fresh bear dung and proactively leading the group to decide to retreat to safer ground.

As individuals who strive to achieve our full potential we may want to assess our strengths, then adjust them to be more in alignment with recent organizational changes. To assist you with assessing your own proficiency in this area, mark an X on the continuum at the point you currently see yourself in the workplace (1 low and 10 high).

Remain calm and open-minded during collaborative efforts with others.

1_____5_____10

Perceived by others as friendly in my initial contact with other new people.

1_____5_____10

Considered a steady, reliable team member who is not prone to extreme moodiness.

1_____5_____10

Models trustworthy behavior towards others by sharing power and responsibilities.

1_____5_____10

When participating in self-empowered work teams, often emerge as a group leader.

1_____5_____10

Often performs best group work when a sense of security exists in sharing information and expertise openly.

1_____5_____10

Confront others' unacceptable behavior in a highly professional and respectful manner.

1_____5_____10

When leading team efforts, view members as a talent pool of people with a variety of expertise to offer.

1_____5_____10

When working with others, has the inclination to seek creative or innovative solutions to problems.

1_____5_____10

Model for others a tolerance for ambiguity in the early stages of problem solving.

1_____5_____10

Considered an approachable, flexible team player who has proven ability in successfully shifting roles and responsibilities when needed.

1_____5_____10

Proven ability to approach projects with an optimistic long-range vision regarding successful team efforts.

1_____5_____10

You may find it informative to go back to the beginning and mark an O along the continuum where you believe others at work perceive your skill level to be. The significant discrepancies between the X's and

O's will provide you with important food for thought.

One of my favorite quotes on self-reliance is from Louisa May Alcott, "I am not afraid of storms, for I am learning how to sail my own ship." I have learned that I can, when it is desperately needed, even build my ship while sailing it.

Demonstrate Effective Interpersonal Communication Skills

Effective interpersonal communication skills are vital to successful careers. This is not just true for trapeze artists in their place of work, but for all of us trying to help our companies grow and remain highly competitive in today's ever-changing marketplace. Using clear verbal and written communication makes it possible for others to readily and accurately understand your ideas, messages, and information.

Effectual communication at work takes time, ingenuity, and a concentration on purpose. For some of us, these are the very factors that trigger our automatic response into the "delegate mode." As tempting as it is, resist! The truth is: there is not anyone left to delegate our tasks to with today's smaller, streamlined workforce. Times have changed. Today it is challenging even for CEO's to get their company's story told correctly to the media. The recent increase in electronic mail, voice-mail, distance learning, and video conferencing provides many new tools with which you are to accomplish this goal. Strengthening essential interpersonal communication skills may actually be easier than you think.

Clear and Concise Communication

"I would write you a short letter if I had the time."

— Abe Lincoln

As a child, others labeled me as bossy. Even at an early age, I put a different spin on it and called it "leadership." In the classroom I was always in trouble for enthusiastically calling out the answers to the teacher's questions. I remember being surprised by her show of displeasure, in view of the fact that I always raised my hand as I called out. Looking back, I recognize that there were some wiser kids in that classroom who seemed to know something that I did not. However, it remained a mystery to me into adulthood. In my early thirties I found myself taking the time to reflect on my performance at work. I was shocked to discover that what I considered my strength was also my weakness: effective communication . . . the listening part. How could that be? This was a humbling experience. Nevertheless, over the following years I learned to be a much better listener. I did not take a course in paying attention or in eavesdropping. I began talking less and listening more. It was my intense desire to improve that drove me to begin seriously observing the behaviors of others who were highly accomplished in the area of effective communication.

In addition to listening skills, many of my current clients are identifying and targeting their own personal set of skills to strengthen. The rapid changes in their job roles and responsibilities at work are often behind their feeling a sense of urgency. They report significant changes in management's expectations of high performance in areas such as:

- Serving as an internal coach or mentor to others
- Quickly building rapport and trust with new customers
- Membership on new high-powered, self-directed work teams
- Training and educating employees with measurable results
- Presenting important project updates to key stakeholders
- Communicating internally via increased meetings, publications, messages
- Building strong partnerships and alliances with other organizations
- Chairing or individually contributing to vital decision-making meetings
- Providing continuous constructive feedback to their employees regarding performance

I often agree with the great economist Stephen Leacock as he stated a century ago, "I am a great believer in luck and the harder I work the more I have of it." However, it has been pure luck that I ran across good friends, colleagues, and clients who were on the same quest as I towards self-improvement and personal leadership. Our discussions often include the topic of clear communication. At times, when sharing our experiences and thoughts with each other, I believe I can actually feel the heat of that little lightbulb going on over my head when suddenly experiencing that "AhHa!" of understanding. Others in our group have related similar experiences, although without seeing little lightbulbs. We discovered that, in addition to our observing individuals who are highly skilled in an area, sharing our varied work experiences, creatively brainstorming together, and welcoming diverse perspectives on topics have all helped in our search for straightforward solutions to urgent problems.

Ensuring Clear Communication

- Be clear in your own mind about what you want to communicate. Taking a moment to ask yourself the purpose of your next e-mail, meeting, proposal, or presentation will keep you focused.

- Communicate to maximize understanding of your thoughts. Remember that the effectiveness of your communication often correlates with the congruency between verbal and nonverbal messages.

- Deliver your message as concisely as possible. As Abe Lincoln pointed out, this may take more time but will be well worth it.

- When providing performance feedback, describe behavior and situations to others rather than judging them. Stay professional. Employees are more likely to commit to changing their behavior or trying a new approach when told in a tactful, honest, yet respectful manner.

- Understand that facial expressions such as an eyebrow flash, eye contact, and a sincere smile often send a message of "connectedness." Over the years, I have met a number of young children who were not old enough to read words, yet were highly skilled at reading the facial expressions of the adults around them.

- Remember that getting across the meaning of a message is crucial, but your ability to enhance retention is also important. Many memorable messages clearly make sense and often provide information about expectations, rules, desired actions, or requirements.

- When working in groups it is important to establish an environment that welcomes all members to speak up and share information and expertise openly. To ensure that all members are in the loop, you must genuinely demonstrate consistency in your authenticity and trustworthiness.

- Delivering the essential part of a message at the beginning is often a sensible approach. Before you press your computer send button, take time to make sure a clear, concise message will be sent. To achieve results or encourage action, it may be wise to cover one topic per e-mail.

- Your positive body language while listening and speaking says to others that they matter and their contributions are valued.

Final Thoughts

Yes, the basic principle behind the motto "Be Prepared" still holds true today. Once adopting this approach to your own career development, you will be ready to thrive in the midst of change when it happens again in the near future . . . and it will!

Knowledge and understanding of key practices desired in today's workplace and the current business needs that drive them is just the first step in preparing yourself to remain a valuable contributor to your company. The second step is applying this knowledge by practicing new behaviors. Finally, the third step is becoming a dependable change agent in the workforce, whose behavior demonstrates a high level of competency in working with others, in communicating information and ideas, in computer savvy, in the ability to prepare and plan ahead, and in creative problem-solving. . . "You are the strongest link — STAY!"

ABOUT
CHERYL MOSER, PH.D.

*C*heryl Moser is a consultant, trainer, and accomplished speaker in areas of change management, leadership competencies, and in organizational development for both the business and educational communities. Her educational background is in social psychology with focus on the workplace. With strong credentials in social science, Cheryl helps individuals unfold, not mold, themselves to make successful workplace transitions and to meet their full potential by developing their own personal leadership. Her experience includes work in areas of management consulting, instructional design, business development, facilitating school improvement teams, career/psychological assessments, and as a national specialist in turning around gifted underachievers. Cheryl is a member of the American Society for Training & Development, International Association of Career Management Professionals, and the National Speakers Association. In addition to consulting, keynoting, and seminars, Cheryl provides interactive web-based learning and cyber-coaching. She is an action-oriented consultant who welcomes technology as a tool in the workplace.

Contact information:
Cheryl Moser, Ph.D.
Cheryl Moser & Associates
P.O. Box 130963
Birmingham, AL 35213-0963
Phone: (205) 871-8644
Fax: (205) 879-8027
E-mail: Cheryl@CherylMoser.com
Website: www.CherylMoser.com

The Power of Politeness in the Midst of Change

by Carolyn Millet

Since its birth, America has been in the midst of change. What part has politeness, or the lack of it, played in our ever evolving society?

What Holds Us Together

Two things that allow us to live as a polite society are order and respect. Without order and without respect, there is no harmony. Without harmony, our lives seem to be disjointed, and it takes more energy to get things done. The end of each day finds us stressed, angry, and exhausted.

Let's Look at History

America is more than just a nation. When you read about and understand the Revolutionary War, you come to realize our forefathers were fighting to uphold their ideas of what a nation could be. The history books tell us that our country was founded on freedom — freedom that had its roots imbedded in order and respect. At that time, there were not many laws as we know them. What prevailed were the rules of religion, civility, and morality. Over the past fifty years, politeness and civility have taken a severe beating, and what has emerged are anger and rudeness. Many of our older citizens are shaking their heads and wondering how this happened.

World War II showed us what occurs when a culture is dehumanized. The lesson of what happened in Germany came home, and as a result America was determined to create a more civil society in which the rights of all people were respected. The 1950's saw many changes. Corporations sought out employees for the long term, creating a sense of security. Marriage and families were treated with more respect. Divorce was rare. The 1950's were geared to commitment, habit, and custom. All of this gave us anchors. We were operating under the rules of civility and politeness. Today we place these values in the realm of choice.

The decline of politeness, order, duty, respect, and even responsibility began in the 60's. Something as simple as standing up when the judge enters the courtroom was seen as a rule to be challenged. The younger generation did not make the rule, and, therefore, did not see the need to abide by it. Civil disobedience became a revolution. Many of the Baby Boomers, born between 1946 and 1964, decided to remake America to suit them. We saw it in their behavior, dress, and beliefs. They sent signals of nonconforming to religion by not attending services, to society by their dress code and free ideas of sex and drugs, and to government by burning draft cards and looking for deferments. The word freedom was taken to a new level. Freedom came to mean "do your own thing" with not much concern for the feelings of anyone else. Individuality and self-centeredness became the norm. This attitude continued to grow throughout the 70's, 80's, and 90's. Society did not challenge them by saying this was not acceptable. At first, members of the older generation were shocked, but as time went on, they became numb and ignored it. Did they think it was just a phase of youth? Did they really believe that one day they would wake up, and order would be restored? An entire generation was allowed to push the limits of politeness and social graces that were the very core of the American ideal. The long-lasting effect of this behavior has been less formality with no clear-cut guidelines for social order. This informality has permeated our communities, our families, and our government. It has unraveled the fabric of our dignity as a society. We have become a nation of rude people.

What Makes Us Rude Today

On top of the freedom to be rude, add technology. This means more freedom at a faster pace, with greater competition, more isolation, and no rules. What a scary combination. In the past, as each piece of modern technology evolved, there was time to develop the social graces that would go with it. It took 30,000 years to develop the written word as a means of formal communication. Prior to that, everything was verbal. Family history was passed down through oral stories. In the past fifty years, we have added the television and VCR, improved the telephone, added the answering machine, call waiting, call return, and Caller ID. A few short years ago, the fax machine was at the forefront of technology. Today it is the Internet, laptops, and cell phones. It seems the focus is on technology and not on people.

Cell phones are both the blessing and curse of modern society. Granted, they have helped close business deals, saved lives as well as time, and kept us in contact with loved ones. It is always helpful to know when the spouse or significant other is only a few minutes from home so you know when to put the steaks on the grill, or so that you can call and say, "On your way home will you stop and pick up milk for tomorrow's breakfast." I am all for it. However, we frequently use the convenience without any thought to courtesy.

Cell Phone Courtesy

1. Turn off cell phone when:
- In a meeting
- In places of worship
- Visiting friends in a hospital
- Cultural events, e.g. the symphony, the theater, even the movies
- Having lunch with a friend or for business

2. Private conversations need to be held in private
- Excuse yourself from the table or group

3. Stop shouting

People have yet to realize the difference between having a person-to-person conversation, and having a cell phone conversation. When speaking person-to-person, you speak in a lower tone, and the other person responds accordingly. This tone and volume matches the tone and volume of other people around you having conversations. Because this interaction flows in harmony with the surrounding chatter, you really do not hear anyone else's conversation. However, when you break that harmony with a loud one-way conversation into a cell phone, you call attention to yourself, and people cannot help but eavesdrop on your conversation.

Modern Technology and Anger

Our labor-saving devices have played a major role in increasing the speed of our lives and the level of attack on politeness and civility. We no longer see people face to face. We have become obscure, and in that obscurity, have taken the liberty to be rude. We leave messages on answering machines that we would never say in person. We hide behind anonymity and send attacking e-mails.

What a cheap shot. If I don't know you, or if I can't see you, I don't have to be polite to you! This comes from a generation of people who did not learn how to treat others with honor, respect, or dignity. This new technology has created isolation and with it the belief that people can set their own rules. It is another version of "do my own thing." It is a "me first," selfish attitude that comes from not learning how to play by the rules of order and respect Freedom without boundaries, civility, or rules, undermines humanity and brings it down to the lowest common denominator.

Anger and the eruption of powerful feelings have become acceptable and normal behavior in our society today. Expressing uncontrolled anger can be quite dangerous. Those people who are not erupting in anger are fearful of those who are. We once used shame as a controlling factor to unruly behavior. Not many would want to embarrass themselves by acting in a way that would cause people to look at them with a disapproving stare. It was a stare that sent with it the message that the behavior, the body language, the gesture, or the force was not acceptable, and you needed to get yourself in check quickly. When the shame is removed, and there is no controller, the door opens to a culture of anger and violence. Today, people are afraid to step up and say, "Excuse me, you can't do that." Instead of getting involved, people are fearful of getting sued or getting hurt if they take a stand. With this attitude, everyone loses.

The children of some of the parents that work in my office building go there every day after school. They range from elementary to high school age. Instead of latchkey kids, we have office children. The problem began when they would hang out in the small lobby, talk loud, bang on the vending machines, or run down the halls. Office workers would complain to each other but not say anything to the children. No one wanted to step up and say, "Excuse me, your behavior in this office building is not acceptable." One day, I decided this had to stop. It was obvious the parents were not going to come out and say anything. I walked down the hall and into the lobby. I said, "Excuse me, ladies and gentlemen; you are in an office building, not on the school ground. You may not holler at each other or even talk loud. Your voices carry down the hall and interrupt business. Also you may not bang on the vending machine or use obscene language. If the machine has taken your money, write down all the information needed, and I will see that you get reimbursed the next time the man fills the machine." I said it simply, but firmly. That has been a few months ago, and no further incidents have occurred. In fact, if they are in the lobby when I come into the building, we exchange hello's. These young people simply needed to be told that they were in a place where rules and respect existed. They need to be there, and we need to conduct business. Now we do that in harmony. This was a polite way of using shame as a controlling factor to unruly behavior. I believe that people are basically good, and it is our duty to teach, guide, and raise the bar whenever the opportunity presents itself. You cannot wait for someone else to do it.

When my sister and I were growing up, the controller was our mother. If we were misbehaving in any way, shape or form, Mother would give us "The Look." It was a look that would stop us cold at fifty paces. It was a look that sent the silent message "what you are doing is unacceptable, don't embarrass me or yourself," and of course, "we will talk about this when we get home." I do not see today's parents giving "The Look" to their children. Why not? Children want to know the rules, and they will push until they find the boundaries. In every sport, there are rules. When a player does not follow the rules, there is a consequence either for the team or the player. Because we have kept our rules in sports, we have organized play.

Why have we put the rules of sports above our rules of social behavior? I teach social skills and ballroom dance to sixth, seventh, and eighth grade boys and girls. I cannot tell you how many times parents have told me their child cannot participate in this class because it conflicts with a sports practice. Social skills class is once a month, and sports practice is three times a week. Look where we have put our values. Over time these choices have led us to rudeness. We are not teaching the next generation how to live under the rules of order and respect; therefore, we perpetuate the "me first" attitude.

What Role Does The Family Play?

I see the family as the key ingredient to bringing us back to a polite society. It begins with us as a parent or a relative. What kind of role model are we? Children learn what they live. If they grow up seeing us out of control, they will learn that is permissible, and they will be out of control. If they hear bad language, they will get the message that it is O.K. for them also. How much television does your child watch? Are the programs monitored for quality, or are they programs that undermine respect for the sake of a laugh? The computer is a great tool for learning. However, allowing our children to use the computer for long hours of entertainment, promotes isolation, poor posture, and poor social skills. In order to teach our children, we must interact with them.

How many times a day do children hear, or use, the six most powerful phrases in the English language: "Please, Thank You, You're Welcome, May I, Excuse Me, I'm Sorry"? These are powerful words because they have the ability to make changes in our family life and our communities. When you bump into someone, you make the decision to say, "Watch where you're going," or to say, "Excuse me." You have the power to make a difference. Courtesy is not rocket science. The truth is, courtesy is so simple that people overlook its value.

Training in good manners that begins in the home helps young people build self-esteem and self-confidence in order to make a more seamless integration into the community. When people have self-esteem, they are more respectful of themselves and therefore more respectful of others. There is no need to be rude, or violent, because the emphasis is on building character.

Social skill improvement is necessary for ourselves and our community. The more we learn and practice the small courtesies of life, the higher we raise our standard of living. Something as simple as recognizing the existence of another individual with a smile has the power to change a person's day. It is hard to be angry when someone is being kind to you. When we change our thinking from "me first," to putting other people first, we get back more than we think we are giving up. That is the Law of the Universe. When you are in the checkout line with a full grocery cart, be aware of the person behind you who has only a few items. Let him or her go ahead of you, and watch the smile. What a reward! How about being a little nicer when driving on our streets and highways. What can you do to eliminate road rage? Is it truly so important for you to get there first, that you must be rude to someone else? It is sad that we have put the emphasis on speed and technology, and in doing so, we have dehumanized people. These are not the principles for which our fore-fathers fought. As a nation, we have prospered and grown because of change. However, we need not lose sight of the fact that we are people first, and to live in harmony, we have certain needs.

Our basic and primary need is to slow down and be kind to each other. We were not designed to live life at a frantic pace, which places a lot of strain on the body and causes disease, illness, and breakdown. Ghandi said, "The purpose of life was not to increase its speed." Take time to know your neighbors, smile at strangers, and make those six power phrases, mentioned earlier, a part of your vocabulary. When this behavior becomes a part of you, I am certain you will notice that your world has become a nicer place.

Summary

You Evoke Change When You

1. Practice cell phone courtesy

    • Know when it is polite to turn off your cell phone

2. Get involved

    • Take a stand

    • Be part of the solution, not the problem

3. Become a good role model

    • Practice honor, dignity and respect toward others
    Our children are watching

4. Change your thinking

    • Alter the "me first" attitude

    • Show courtesy to others

Manners are the happy way of living.

ABOUT
CAROLYN MILLET

*C*arolyn Millet, a popular expert on etiquette, works with companies who want to learn how manners make money, and politeness affects profits. As she describes it, "This is a low tech method for obtaining high tech results in customer relations, management and sales." Her workshops are packed with practical advice on how to motivate people, build teamwork, and promote harmony in the workplace through the use of politeness. To help adults with their table manners, she offers evening classes in "Dining Like a Diplomat" on how to talk and eat your way through a five-course meal with confidence. Carolyn also works with young people. In the San Francisco area, Carolyn teaches social skills, manners, and ballroom dance to 6th, 7th, and 8th grade boys and girls. By calling them "ladies and gentlemen," she sets the tone for their journey into adulthood. Carolyn is a member of Toastmasters International and the National Speakers Association.

Contact information:
Carolyn Millet
Power of Politeness
P.O. Box 7058
Burlingame, CA 94011
Phone: (650) 340-9862
Fax: (650) 340-1287
E-mail: Carolyn@Polite.com
Website: www.Politeness.com

WHAT IS YOUR
CATALYST FOR CHANGE?

by Michelle Cubas

How often do you catch yourself "swatting-flies"? Can you hear the buzzing now? Swatting flies is similar to the overloaded thinking activity that swirls in our expanding heads. This swirling creates a buzzing, and we feel like our brains are plugged into an electric socket! This buzzing occurs when we haven't defined information. The meaning hasn't surfaced outside of our heads, and we haven't written it down!

Part of this "swatting-flies" phenomenon is due to the fact that our biology has not kept pace with our technology. We're overwhelmed and over stimulated by decibels and pixels that our eyes and ears were never intended to process.

Consider our daily exposures:

- Too much external stimuli. Constant bombardment of sound pollution, elected or otherwise.

- Inability to process and assimilate information creates Info Anxiety.™

- Not enough rest time.

- Lack of focus due to distractions; fueled by *shoulds*, *have to's* and *judgment*.

- Active pursuit of other's ideas, not our own, creates Seepage™ and energy drain.

- Exposure to deliberate misinformation clouds personal

judgment like urban legends, jokes on email, plausible denia-
bility leaks, etc.

What does this have to do with a catalyst for change? Simply, there
is another way to live; you always suspected there might be. Follow me
. . . for a sneak peek into alternatives to *contempobabble,*™ the buzz of
contemporary living.

The Power of Words

It begins with the power of our language. Immediately, you can use
what is familiar and what you already know. Little effort is required
here. For a start, let's consider these words.

- Catalyst (noun) *The causing or acceleration of a chemical
  change by the addition of a substance, which is not permanently affected by the reaction.*

- Change (verb transitive) 1. to make different; alter in condition, appearance, turn; 2. to *substitute* another or others in
  exchange for something else.

The second definition offers us power. It offers us an exit from the
anxiety many people experience when thinking about "altering a condition or appearance."

What Is the Alternative?

Here are two easy, positive tools.

1. Substitute the word *shift* for *change* in your vocabulary. It will
   feel strange at first. However, you will be conscious of using
   it, which is what you want to achieve.

2. Use *choice* as the motivation for *shifting*. We get to *choose*
   what needs to be done, and then assign a response rather than
   feeling victimized by the situation.

Definition two is powerful because it releases us from the associated words, feelings, and connotations that come with the word
"change." Let's use an image here. By shifting, we can associate with
driving a stick-shift car and having the power to move freely through the
sequence of shifting! Another benefit of shifting is the association with

movement and direction. Then, we can avoid "seepage."

Without active shifting, we experience what I call Seepage. Seepage is the physical experience of feeling life and energy slipping out and away from you, not by your own choosing; you feel a lack of control, "floating anxiety," and extreme vulnerability. Seepage causes exhaustion, futility, negativity, and spiritual drought. It creates complacency. *Complacency is the sludge blocking creativity,*™ like plaque on our teeth. Instead of consciously shifting, we are swept away by external forces and perceive we have nothing to do with the "sweeping!" Suggested substitute words to use: shift, move, leap, suppose, consider, what if it works?

Definition two offers us freedom from feeling victimized. Dr. Robert Schuller, global motivational speaker and pastor of the Crystal Cathedral in Orange County, California, said, "We can't always choose our circumstances, but we can always choose our response to them." This thought releases freedom and provides a stimulus for creativity. It is also a handy mantra when life is not going the way we would like.

Interestingly, the very people uncomfortable with change are often the same people that tell me they are not creative. This self-proclaimed "uncreative state" tells me several truths about the speaker:

- The person has difficulty visualizing or has never practiced doing it.
- The person wasn't encouraged to draw out of the lines in the coloring book.
- The person has little if any experience using imagination.
- The person values conformity.

On the flip side, if complacency is sludge, then creativity requires involvement and energy.

Creativity is boundless. It is expressed in many forms, not just the arts. Quick assessment, talent with numbers and problem-solving skills are forms of creativity. Creativity is the mother of change; the act of creativity creates change. The relationship between creativity and change is symbiotic.

We have to participate. Being involved with a creative process serves us in finding solutions to our everyday challenges that are often manifested in an inability to communicate our needs. This can fester and become frenzy. After all, creativity and energy are not enough to temper our modern lifestyles.

My explanation for our modern frenzy is simple. We need to activate our language in order to express all that we are feeling. On any given day we can feel like an 18-month-old child beginning verbal language. We experience frustration. The lack of verbal expression stirs emotion which overtakes/dominates our experience. The emotion becomes our memory and transports that emotion to the present activity. People are limited by a lack of vocabulary to express what they imagine; their creativity is not limited, just their verbal expression.

Simply, we are over stimulated by noise, caffeine, drugs, alcohol, and pollution. We can't process so many distractions. Consider that over stimulation stifles the Muse (creativity) that yearns for personal expression. We confuse the Muse with self-indulgence because we haven't identified who the Muse is or how to become acquainted with the Muse. How does that make you feel? Please stop for a moment. Write down how you are responding right now. Use one or two words _____.

Practice

As an exercise, step into a sports bar, eatery marked "grille," or nightclub and experience the distraction from seven television screens, loud music, and people screaming to be heard. The noise has an effect of drowning for me!

The setting can be likened to many ancient traditions where people deliberately put themselves into a stupor to evoke euphoria. It simultaneously had physiological and psychological effects. The overload is a catalyst; it imposes change on the participants, and they can release responsibility to the circumstances. Think of possible social or cultural reasons the scene is set like that.

- Impersonal
- Non-involvement
- Non-conversational
- Add your own: _____

Practice Shifting

- Start by imagining a box of crayons.
- How many crayons are in the box?
- Pick a color. Be specific; is it red, pink, rose, etc.? That's visualization.
- Now blend two colors to create a third color. (Hint: blue + red = purple)
- You pick your own combination.

Another Easy Practice

- Close your eyes for a moment.
- Look upward toward the center of your forehead, your Mind's Eye.
- Visualize a second floor landing with a railing and banister leading to the stairway.

Next . . . Follow the stairway down from the landing. The stairway is on which side of the landing?

Next . . . You are at the bottom of the stairs. Now write down which way you turn and into which part of the house you are entering. This simple practice will stimulate and free you to use what you already have — an imagination and powers!

Dorothy, in Frank Baum's *Wizard of Oz*, had powers, too. She had the ruby slippers from the opening of the story; she just didn't know how to activate or use them. Her journey on the yellow brick road was self-*discovery* and learning how to trust herself. On her path, she bumped into reminders of what was necessary for a balanced and healthy life while creatively seeking a way to *wisdom*.

The tin man (heart), scarecrow (brains) and cowardly lion (courage) already possessed what they were seeking. The characters already exhibited the sought-after qualities. It wasn't until they found someone/something to care more about than themselves that the awareness became clear. What the characters really needed was validation. The story's end provided the external validation. They realized they had to validate themselves.

The lesson from this story can be that we want to build on our inner wisdom, what we already know and welcome in additional knowledge that can keep us free and provide future options. Otherwise, we're trapped.

Simple Option Boosters:

- Read whatever you can get your hands on. The eye-hand relationship of reading is strongly connected to the imagination.
- Limit electronic visual stimuli while you are developing this process.
- Stimulate your Mind's Eye by gazing out a window. Notice the play of light, the colors, the emotion of the moment.

Simple Mastery™ —Begin simply—Simply begin.™ It works! It takes practice. It will change your Universe.

Who Is Minding Your Life?

When I ask seminar participants about their perception of who runs their universe, the room goes silent. Many assign their deity to the task of puppeteering their every personal move and event. Many don't feel any control or part in living their own lives.

What's at work here?

- It's a set-up or sabotage.
- Control is an illusion.
- Control is an absolute word like "perfection."
- Absolutes are unattainable.

This set-up relates to a common perception that change happens *to* us. *Change* is the noun form of the word used the subject of the clause.

I suggest we use the verb form and say something like, "I will change my _____." With this statement, we become responsible for the doing.

Substitute the word "mastery" instead of "control." How does it affect your thinking? Use it in your writing and speaking. It takes a bit of practice. The first step is being aware of it. Remember, we're going for mastery, not control.

• It is measurable.

• Mastery is attainable.

• It is ongoing and evolving without a destination, only an appointed direction.

Practice: Write two rules that everyone who enters your universe MUST follow.

1. _____.
2. _____.

Mastery Offers Abundant Benefits

Consider these. They are 3 'I's:

1. *Increased* satisfaction, health and well-being

2. *Improved* role models for future generations

3. *Incentive* to build, construct, and admire our work, markers that we were here (pyramids, towers, monuments)

The mind is the ultimate idea assimilator!™ Once we shift our perception and make change happen, we are no longer victims enduring our lot in life or killing time.

Role Models for Change

An instant way to begin shifting is to read about how others have handled situations. We want to tread in the steps of Leonardo da Vinci, Michelangelo, Isaac Stern, Golda Meir, Margaret Thatcher, Indira Ghandi, Winston Churchill, Ansel Adams, and Henry David Thoreau. What can we borrow from their experience? Who is your role model?

Read about these people and why they stand apart from the crowd.

Distinguish what they did. Which practice or idea of theirs sets them apart from everyone else (in your family, community, country)? Since you know the historical reference and often the outcome, think through the characteristics within these models that helped them to achieve those outcomes. Choose one aspect of these great people. Apply it to yourself. For example, Leonardo da Vinci kept multiple journals, notes, and doodles. He took naps during the day. He was a vital human being even as he aged. How would some of his habits serve you?

Playing (yes, playing!) with Legos® and building blocks, cross-word puzzles and doodle books, word search and jigsaw puzzles, all stimulate creativity and creativity's result — change, a shift. Your mind becomes ready to receive these changes and doesn't resist when you introduce new combinations of thoughts. Actually, preparing the mind to receive information is the foundation of dynamic reading training like *Evelyn Wood Reading Dynamics.*™

Any Procrastinators?

Procrastination is stubborn, fear-based resistance to change. Procrastinators perceive the act of procrastination as their only limited option. They actually use different catalysts to move off the mark. (See 1-3 below.)

Each of the following represents a coping mechanism by the user. Often, these are learned techniques from family members, caretakers, and life experiences that are adapted by the procrastinator as personal coping skills. A key to these perceptions is that the presence or source of power lies outside oneself.

Types of procrastination:

1. *Deadline driven* — The adrenaline "rush" of being close to the wire becomes a form of motivation and forces the procrastina-tor to make a move. Deep breathing and "flight" response serve as fuel to action. The user has a bloated sense of heroism when sliding into the deadline. It is yet another test of worthi-ness and capability for the user. Useful antidotes: Time man-agement and organizational training.

2. *Avoidance/Ignorance* — Lack of information, judgment, and not knowing are the armor of the person waiving the right to be responsible for personal actions. This type of procrastination limits new data from entering and offering possibilities. The users are dependent only on what they perceive around them instead of drawing upon their inner resources. Useful antidotes: Puzzles and problem solving with cause and effect and relationship practices.

3. *Paralysis* (the deer in the headlights image) — This response is often accompanied by shallow breathing and an inability to effectively assess a real or perceived threat. The response can be phobic and debilitating in its extreme form. The fear of change is stronger than the need to move off a mark, move away from an abusive situation or move up or out! Useful antidotes: Simple imagination development and breathing exercises. Once they learn that they "lived" through the imagined circumstance, they can use those tools again. What they can learn from that experience will be helpful in overcoming paralysis.

The key to shifting away from procrastination resides in the person's ability to constructively express what the fear is.

Consider this . . . Your perception is the final filter through which you assess, judge, react, respond, think and decide about everyone and everything in your Universe!

Pick A Catalyst

Consider O-Principle™ Dynamics — Openmindedness + Options = Opportunities or better known in my Universe as *Getting ready to Meet your Greatness!*™ It's a game. The more open your mind, the more you see options; the visual field opens. The more options you perceive, the more your personal risk factor drops. More opportunities create expanded possibilities. It is a positive self-fulfilling prophecy. ***More Catalytic Samples to Ponder...***

Openmindedness — Invent the direction. Play "what if" scenarios. Take each to a logical conclusion. Which one appeals to you the most?

Options (Choices) — Navigate, map, and set the path.

- Write three steps to the "what if" scenarios
- Put them in priority order — A,B,C.
- Create a realistic timing that's doable within your universe.
- Describe how you will launch this element.

Direct — This is the *Risk Factor*. It requires you to take action using three phases: Implement-Monitor-Adjust.

- Set your actions into place.
- Monitor the progress.
- Make periodic, planned adjustments before conditions are out of alignment.

Admire — Appreciate the opportunities you have created.

- Fill yourself with the feeling of each accomplishment.
- Consider how you met the moments that called forth the best in yourself.
- Remember the little colored and gold stars you received in school when you did your best. Build on these feelings.

Here are five catalytic steps to set you on your path and begin your map — I.N.D.I.A.

- Invent
- Navigate
- Direct
- Implement
- Admire Your Accomplishments

Draw your map here: (a flow chart or outline works well)

Describe it here . . .

_____

_____

_____

_____

Try This Sample Plan . . .

- Assess — What needs to be different from the outset?
- Assert — Stand for the values you represent. Define what they are.
- Assign Value — to your accomplishments. (Draw symbols that mean something to you; use stickers, colors, jewels, scenery, paint.) Preset your Reward Range. e.g. A preset range of 'A' may be a trip, 'B' a spa treatment, or 'C' a book at your favorite bookstore. What holds value for you?

    You can use this three-step plan in your professional and personal relationships as well as individually. Also, the plan is pleasing to children. They particularly like choosing the ranges. It helps them make choices and visualize a goal direction. Also, you can teach your staff this easy plan and reap the benefits: improved self-reliance, reduced interruptions, and increased initiative within your team.

Cues to Consider

Another catalytic signal is when you find yourself in the position to negotiate your position on a topic, situation, or opinion. Feeling like you have to cling to your position? Most adults don't have the experience or exposure to conduct effective negotiations. For practice, read Herb Cohen's *You Can Negotiate Anything* or listen to audio tapes and learn the language of persuasion. Or, just watch toddlers who want to stay up after being put to bed. Children are masterful negotiators. They don't perceive a threat of losing anything until the threat is presented by the exhausted parent!

How can we apply this "nothing-to-lose" attitude to ourselves?

Can we identify the very emotion? Can it be the fear of loss that motivates us to dig in our heels? A fear to explore what else we want? What are we hiding? Are we afraid of coming up empty-handed, being bullied, being overlooked? Instead of psychoanalyzing the situation, let's ask ourselves, "What must I do/see/think differently in order to achieve my desired results?"

Tips for Power Negotiating

- Pick neutral surroundings when possible.
- What is reasonable to expect?
- Never take the first offer.
- Stay away from "losing ground" scenarios.
- Focus on mutual results.
- Avoid power plays.
- Take 'You' out of the process.
- Know in advance what concessions are acceptable from your perspective instead of stewing about giving things up.

The Pay Off — Long-Term Benefits

Once you master negotiation skills, you will notice you have less of a desire for competitive stands. It's like having a mental black belt in karate. You will respect and allow others to have their points of view. You will no longer need to be "right." You will become more open-minded which will stimulate your imagination and creativity. You will release the freedom associated with creativity because your energy isn't holding on to an outcome. The more freedom, the greater the creativity, which, in turn, leads to greater freedom!

Mastery Offers Abundant Benefits

- Remember your role models for change and new habits.
- Consider the 3 'I's — Increased satisfaction, health and well-being; Improved role models for future generations; Incentive to build, construct, and admire our work.
- Create Your Plan. You are then assured of having a place to

return when there is a swerve or when a different gate opens.

- Consider O-Principle™ Dynamics — Openmindedness + Options = Opportunities
- I.N.D.I.A.— five catalytic steps to freedom.
- Negotiate your way to confidence and peace in your life.
- Build your vocabulary by reading every day. You will be better able to express exactly what you mean and build your confidence.

The next time you feel the "painted-into-a-corner" mood coming on, or you have over thought a scenario, consider this eloquent paraphrasing — a thought from Albert Einstein. He states that we can never find a solution to a problem in the same environment in which it was created.

Simply step back, step up, or step to the side, and you'll experience your perspective changing. PRACTICE, and come to recognize that reassuring feeling of choosing your response. You can call upon it at your will. You WILL find that you have the power to click those ruby slippers!

ABOUT
MICHELLE CUBAS

As a speaker, consultant, and writer, Michelle Cubas focuses on issues of competency in the new economy, with special emphasis on written, technical, and verbal business language skills. her "Proprietary Business Literacy Tactics" are applied with laser precision. She instructs on preparation and delivery for important presentations, and customizes materials to brand business messages for internal and external audiences. She sees her objective as raising an organization's overall learning pace, especially in areas of leadership, call center services, and sales and territory development. Together, these key areas enhance loyalty, increase results, and bridge existing operational gaps. All programs are tailored to match each organization's unique needs. Some of her popular topics include: "How Do I Get People To Do What I Want Them To Do?," "Build Equity into Your Business Beyond the Bottom Line!," "Create a Catalyst for Painless Change!," and "Put Power Behind the Force in Work . . . Instill a Platinum Work Ethic!"

Contact information:
Michelle Cubas
Positive Potentials, LLC
7120 E. 6th Avenue, #21
Scottsdale, AZ 85251
Phone: (480) 922-9699
Fax: (480) 663-6851
E-mail: MCubas@PositivePotentials.com
Website: www.PositivePotentials.com

WORKING WITH EMBRACERS, ACCEPTORS, AND AVOIDERS

by Doug Smart, CSP

A new idea will get its first negative response within three seconds. If you are working with polite people, the time for the initial negative response extends to ten seconds. You've seen it happen at staff meetings. Someone tosses out a simple idea, such as streamlining the paperwork by combining two forms, and the rabble begins: "Oh, we can't do that. It will never work. We tried it before, you know, seven years ago. It will be more trouble than it's worth. Good luck trying to get that approved! If it isn't broken, why fix it? Let's study it."

Why such unfriendliness toward a new idea?

Everyone has a comfort zone. Your comfort zone is a lifetime compilation of the learning you have received from every sensation you have had since birth. The things that made you happy have left their mark, as have the things that made you sad, mad, glad, and every other emotion you have experienced. You have learned the hard way that carpet fuzz tastes awful, that people who smile a lot are also capable of lying a lot, and that jumping for a new idea sometimes leaves you worse off than staying married to an old idea. Your comfort zone is a decision-making tool. It provides instant, in-the-gut analysis. The accumulated experiences in your comfort zone have constructed a network of wisdom that helps you make lightning-fast decisions, most of which happen so swiftly you don't realize decisions were made (such as deciding to press the brake at a red light, deleting a junk e-mail, or laughing chummily the moment the boss finishes her joke). Your comfort zone helps you gravitate toward the good you want and stay away from the bad you want to avoid. It helps keep your life on an even keel. That which is familiar, recognizable, and well-known to you is comfortable. Even those things that others might find uncomfortable (such as skydiving or managing 45 salespeople) can provide comfort to you. Your comfort zone wants one thing out of life: comfort. And your comfort zone reacts to protect you when you are faced with the opposite of comfort, which is change.

All change is stressful. Some people react more strongly than others, but you can be certain that change evokes a sensation of discomfort in every comfort zone. There's nothing like the implied change of a bold new idea to grab the attention of your comfort zone.

When it comes to reacting to change, we tend to lay claim to one of three categories: *embracers*, *acceptors*, and *avoiders*. Some people readily accept change, some are willing but cautious, and some give in to an instinctive reaction to resist it. You work with all three types.

Embracers

Psychologists estimate that about 20 percent of people enjoy change. They see it as adventuresome, exciting, and necessary. They like to see things stirred up every now and then. To them, the status quo can become boring, and the cure to dullness is change. In business, an embracer might express herself like this: "Phil, I love your idea, you know, the one you talked about in the meeting today. I've got some questions about procedures and I see where it could hit a couple of snags, but all that can be worked out. Basically, it's such a solid idea, I don't know why we didn't do it your way years ago. Count me in. I'm with you on this." Embracers are not pushovers, but if a new idea makes sense to them and feels right, they are ready to embrace it. Potential negatives to the new idea can be dealt with later, when it is time to iron out the kinks. The people around them tend to see embracers as optimists.

Acceptors

Fifty percent of people are more cautious in their approach. They have more of a "wait and see" attitude. A change acceptor might express himself like this: "Phil, I was thinking about your idea from the meeting. It sounds good and all, but I don't know. I mean, it could work, but there are lots of things to consider. I can see where we could have some big problems. I need to think about this some more. Could you send me something on this? I want to study it. Yeah, send me something and let me look it over. I need to sleep on this. I'll let you know what I decide. Let's talk later." Acceptors are willing to change when their comfort zone is convinced the change is right. These people are fence sitters. They can see both positives and negatives to the new idea. This pull can be immobilizing to anyone, but acceptors sometimes allow one potential negative to counterbalance the advantages of a dozen positives. What they need from you, as the proponent of change, is reassurance. Once you convince them the change is right — through logic (facts, figures, historic examples, reasonable conclusions) or emotion (endorsements, examples, peer acceptance, benefits) — they will likely come to accept the change. Initially the burden is on you to help them feel comfortable that changing is the right course of action. When they are comfortable, they will be convinced.

Avoiders

Thirty percent of people have an aversion to change. When faced with a serious new idea, approximately one out of every three people will hunker down and fight change. Their comfort zones recoil at change and tend to explain change like this: "Change means something is about to be taken away from me. I may not have the greatest thing going, but at least I know what I've got and I'll fight to keep it. I'm not willing to swap my current set of known problems for a new set of unknown problems."

Avoiders, like the others, can be found at any age, education level, and position in business — even upper management. Although they are about 30 percent of the people you work with, they can be expected to generate about 80 percent of the friction on your team. The people who work with them tend to see them as pessimists, although avoiders rarely think of themselves as pessimistic, preferring instead to see themselves as realistic.

Lava Lamps

As you read this, can you see yourself as all three types? Aren't there some new ideas that, to your ears, sound solid, right, and workable? In those instances you are in the 20 percent. But aren't there some new ideas that have you balancing like a seesaw while trying to figure out which way you will decide to shift the weight of your opinion? In those cases you are in the 50 percent. And aren't there some new ideas that are so contrary to your values that, while you politely let the idea presenters talk, your insides are rebelling? "No way! I will never agree to that! You can stop talking right now because there is no way I will support your idea!" It helps to think of lava lamps. The bubbles go up, the bubbles go down. Think of yourself as the biggest bubble and the lava lamp itself as your comfort zone. Upon hearing some ideas, your bubble rises to the top (20 percent). For other ideas you are in the middle (50 percent). And for still others, your bubble settles to the bottom like the dead weight of a stone (30 percent). Through the years, your comfort zone has come to favor one of those three positions more than the other two. When you hear a new idea, you tend to react from one of those three positions more often than the other two. This is how your comfort zone reacts to new ideas. Your natural, typical response is comfortable for you.

Through experience, you have also come to figure out which of the three levels the individuals in your life favor. With a bit of thought, you can probably figure out which of the three your boss usually favors when you bring a new idea to him. The same is true for your spouse, your co-workers, your customers, your kids, your kids' teachers, and everyone else with whom you interact.

Smart Facts You Can Use

As a speaker, I often ask of audiences, "Raise your hand if, in the last 12 months, your professional life has gone through significant change." Whether I'm speaking to people in business, government, healthcare, manufacturing, education, or religion, nearly every hand goes up. It's the same when I ask them if they know anyone back at work who fights change. Then I ask them to holler out the answer to this question, "What percent of people would you guess eventually change?" Many estimate 50 percent to 70 percent, but the real answer is 100 percent. That is good news for you, especially if you have lots of new ideas. It shows that despite resistance, everyone eventually changes. They might not change when you want or the way you want, but everyone changes. That fact shows that momentum favors change agents.

I also like to pose this situation to people: You are in a meeting with co-workers. You have a brand new idea. No one has previously heard your idea. What percent of people can you count on ahead of time to oppose you? Someone always shouts out, "100 percent!" Many say it's 30 percent. But the true answer is 80 percent (that's the 50 percent and the 30 percent ganging up on you).

On the first hearing of a brand new idea, approximately 80 percent of the comfort zones within earshot will suddenly feel bruised. It will be easier (i.e., more comfortable) to repel your idea than it will be to be vulnerable (uncomfortable) by welcoming your new idea.

Do people really reject new ideas readily? Yes. It's human nature. Here's an example. Let's say you go home at the end of a work day. Your significant other meets you at the door and says, "I'm so glad you're home. Look, I had a really rough day. I don't feel like eating at home. Could we go out to eat tonight?"

Let's say the idea sounds okay to you, so you ask, "Where do you want to go?"

"I don't care," significant replies. "Anywhere you want to go is fine with me. I just want to get out."

"Great," you say, "Let's go to that new restaurant by the mall."

And as soon as significant hears those words, significant pauses about three seconds and responds with, "No, I don't want to go there."

On the first hearing of a brand new idea, approximately 80 percent of the people who hear you will fend you off — even the people who love you!

Here are some more interesting facts you can put to use. No matter what your job description says, you are in sales. You are selling your ideas. Actually, you have to sell something very basic to the comfort zones around you before you can even hope to sell your ideas. You have to "sell" — or get them to buy into — this concept: trust me. In order to get your ideas for change into the minds and hearts of others, you have to get past the outer shell of their comfort zones. They have to sense that they can trust you. This is something you know you can't tell people to do because the more you tell or ask people to trust you, the less likely their comfort zones will feel comfortable doing so. You convey trust without specifically asking for it.

Since you are in sales, here's a statistic that can fuel your courage in the face of an adverse reaction to a sweeping new idea you propose. Eighty percent of all expensive, emotion-laden sales (such as buying a house, approving the purchase of a new computer network for the office, or accepting one of your revolutionary ideas) are made after the buyer says "No" five times. That is, it's common for a buyer to reject a trans-action five times before saying "Yes." To give you an example, when we were house hunting, the real estate agent had mailed us pictures of houses. We immediately rejected several, one in particular because it was on the side of a hill and the driveway was very steep. In the course of looking, we couldn't find anything that worked for us and the agent asked us if we would like to see the house on the hill. We agreed, and we liked it a lot, but we turned it down for several reasons. The colonial style was painfully plain. The house needed some redecorating. The driveway was too steep. The price was too high. Despite these short-comings, it had a lot going for it, but it wasn't perfect, so we voiced objections. The agent, sensing this home was right for us, gently and professionally persisted. When we discussed the plainness of the colonial architecture, she pointed out that nearly every house in the area we wanted to live in had a colonial character and that the house fit the neighborhood beautifully. The redecorating could be done later and to our tastes. As for the steep driveway, she simply stated, "You are young." We laughed and agreed. And as to the price, she offered, "I can't speak for the sellers, but if you want to submit a low offer in order to get some discussion started, we could do that." The bottom line is, we signed an offer for a low price and the sellers accepted it. It's been ten years since we bought this house and we love it. The point is, the comfort zones of my wife and me made it easier to say "No" than "Yes" when it was time to make a decision. Thanks to the gentle persistence of the agent, we are in a wonderful house.

What does all this mean to you? Be persistent. When you want others to accept change, don't be too quick to cave in to rejection. Statistically, most salespeople give up at the first whisper of rejection, yet, because of buyers' comfort zones, 80 percent of important sales are made after the fifth "No." When you have a great idea you want others to buy in to, anticipate probable rejection before you get to acceptance. For instance, if you are at a meeting and you courageously throw out a new idea, anticipate at least 80 percent of the people to not immediately embrace your idea. In fact, you might consider that meeting the first of five rejections you will likely face on the journey to acceptance. Philosopher Arthur Schopenhauer understood that it is natural for most people to oppose something before they give in to it. He observed that a new idea goes through these three stages in becoming "the norm":

- First, it is ridiculed.
- Second, it is violently opposed.
- Third, it is accepted as self-evident.

How to Work Effectively with All Types

You can make it easier for other people to accept your ideas by helping their comfort zones be less rigid in the face of change. Here are 34 ideas for working with change embracers, acceptors, and avoiders.

Embracers

- Garner their support before you "go public." Enlist their aid in winning over others

- Solicit their input for improvements and for avoiding potential negative consequences
- Make them part of your team and let their enthusiasm be a guiding light for others
- If qualified, give them lead roles
- Never take them for granted
- Reward their willingness to risk
- Stay loyal to them
- Talk in terms of benefits, both personally and professionally
- Publicly celebrate their successes

Acceptors

- Respect their reluctance and do not attempt to intimidate them into accepting the change
- If appropriate, propose the change as a five-week experiment
- Offer encouragement, reassurance, and training
- Offer evidence and endorsements that support the rationale for the change
- Be honest in your communication, yet err on the side of optimism
- Give them something to believe in
- Show genuine appreciation for their efforts to make the change work
- Don't penalize for "failure." Share success stories and evidence that the change is working as expected (or better)
- For Acceptors who enjoy the spotlight, publicly endorse their personal successes
- Publicly celebrate all successes that validate the change as being the right course for the team

Avoiders

- Try to pinpoint specific reasons for resistance to a particular change

- Listen and try to understand their concerns . . . their pessimism in this case may be well-founded

- Respect that their resistance can be based on both emotion (feelings) and logic (past experiences)

- Discuss worst-case scenarios and contingency plans

- Provide training and opportunities for new positive experiences

- Keep your word

- Partner them with people who have embraced the new idea

- Avoid giving them a high visibility position assuming the change "will bring them around" faster

- Avoid the trap of devoting more energy to this group than to the Embracers and Acceptors

- Accept that it's unlikely you'll gain the support of everyone

- Don't back them into a corner that forces them to "prove" your idea won't work

- Never tolerate insubordination or sabotage that undermines the organization

- If warranted, let them know the consequences of not participating in the change

- Privately acknowledge their individual successes and publicly celebrate group wins.

- In their presence, smile more!

Today Forward

In the past twelve months, significant change has probably impacted your personal and professional lives. The comfort zone, not being a fan of change, will put you, and the people around you, on the defensive and block receptivity to changes that are healthy. How to facilitate positive change? Observe how the people around you habitually respond to change. Expect 20 percent to embrace it, 50 percent to take a non-committed position that may later change to acceptance, and 30 percent to have a "knee-jerk" opposition as they try to avoid the change. Though rejection feels discouraging, take heart in knowing that persistence is an important element in bringing about change.

To help yourself deal effectively with change, be S. M. A. R. T. about change to help guide you through hyper-changing times:

- Stay receptive to change.
- Make people comfortable with change (including yourself).
- Ask clearly for what you want.
- Reward and reinforce new behavior — yours and theirs.
- Try new things often and stay in the rhythm of change.

You won't always be able to sidestep having your new ideas buffeted by a few negative responses within the first three seconds. However, you will be able to put this ice water reception in perspective as natural and predictable as you diffuse the natural resistance comfort zones build against change. Understanding these dynamics of change will help you gain agreement more often to changes you wish to implement — and they will smooth away a lot of the bumps of resistance.

ABOUT
DOUG SMART, CSP

*D*oug Smart, CSP, works with leaders and teams who want to build optimistic organizations and customer loyalty. Clients learn how to bounce back from setbacks, earn customer devotion, and increase business. Plus, they have more fun! Doug is a successful business owner and a former top salesperson who is authoritative and authentic. His daily radio show, "Smarter by the Minute," is heard internationally. He is a consultant, keynoter, and trainer who has spoken at over 1,000 conventions, conferences, seminars, sales rallies, and management retreats. Doug is the author or co-author of* Where There's Change There's Opportunity!, TimeSmart: How Real People Really Get Things Done at Work, Reach for the Stars, Sizzling Customer Service, *and* Brothers Together. *In 1998 the National Speakers Association awarded him the prestigious Certified Speaking Professional designation. Contact Doug's office for an information kit on bringing "The Get Smart Series" of consulting and seminars to your organization.*

Contact information:
Doug Smart, CSP
Doug Smart Seminars
P.O. Box 768024
Roswell, GA 30076
Phone: (770) 587-9784
Fax: (770) 587-1050
E-mail: Doug@DougSmart.com
Website: www.DougSmart.com

CHANGE IS A LEADER'S LAUNCHING PAD

by Tim Bass

C hange is a leader's launching pad. It has been said that in order to be successful you must accept change. I would go a step further; exceptionally successful people not only accept change — they embrace it. They see it as an exciting opportunity instead of a necessary evil. This statement is not meant to imply that all change is exciting and positive; certainly it is not. Some necessary change is inherently negative; however, your response to the change can be positive no matter how negative the circumstances. Habitually positive response to negative situations is a hallmark of highly effective people. Knowing that change is a constant, they prepare for it and are ready to take full advantage when change occurs. Nowhere can this process more clearly be demonstrated than in the area of leadership. Great leaders are almost universally born out of the chaos and disorder of change. Without World War II, Winston Churchill may have gone down in history as an inconsequential government official. Without drastic shifts in the philosophy and methodology of doing business, Jack Welch could never have turned the G.E. Company around with such astonishing results. Without the economic insecurities of the late 70's, Ronald Reagan would likely have never ascended to the most powerful position in the free world. And without the dissolution of a once-proud dynasty, Jimmy Johnson would never have had the opportunity to lead the Dallas

Cowboys to back-to-back Super Bowl titles (okay . . . maybe that doesn't quite compare to the others' accomplishments, but you get the picture). All of these individuals led companies, countries or teams through the minefield of change to remarkable success. Leadership is a coming together of the right set of skills, abilities and circumstances. Change is the mother of those circumstances, and change is a launching pad for leadership.

Prepare Yourself

We know that change is a constant and an absolute. You can be absolutely sure that — no matter what your occupation — something will occur or a set of circumstances will exist that will require significant change in your organization. There will be a merger, a buyout, a downsizing, a shift in methodologies, a revitalization — something that will shake your comfort zone and force a change in the organization. Events such as these turn ordinary leaders into extraordinary ones, and leaders to be born. Therefore, it only makes sense that you should prepare yourself to take advantage of a change in your situation when it arises. This approach is certainly not for everyone. The kind of preparation I am talking about takes commitment. Granted, career strategizing makes some people feel uncomfortable, so please realize that I am not talking about manipulation of people or circumstances to achieve your goals at the expense of other people's needs. I am talking about thinking in advance of opportunity so that you can best act on that opportunity according to your own personal and professional values and beliefs. Thinking ahead and acting according to your values and beliefs is the essence of being proactive rather than reactive, and it shoves some people out of their comfort zones. If you would like to remain comfortable, skip this chapter of the book.

We will first look at preparing and leading organizations in times of change and, in doing so, developing and magnifying yourself as a leader. However, even if you are not a formal leader in your organization at present, the steps and skills we will discuss are just as vital for you in positioning yourself to take advantage of the change to launch yourself into a leadership role. Regardless of the perspective from which you approach change, it is essential that you have a strategy, and that you are creating habits that will serve you when change is necessary. Check yourself in the following four areas to see how well prepared you are to take advantage of the change.

Be the Best Communicator You Know

A survey I sometimes give to my seminar or workshop attendees asks this simple question: "Do you consider yourself a good communicator?" Invariably, about 80 percent of the class responds affirmatively to this question. Later, during the various communication application exercises we go through, I find that roughly 20 percent actually have a high level of communication skills. This communication denial is one of the major reasons people don't work harder on their communication skills. Simply put, your ability to communicate effectively with a variety of people at all levels of an organization will do more to advance your career and raise you into positions of leadership than all other skills combined, no matter what your profession. If you are a doctor, I can assure you that you will lose more patients due to poor bedside manner than lack of skill as a physician. If you are a teacher, your vast knowledge of history, science, or mathematics will be null effect if you do not have a finely honed ability to communicate the information. You will be left with a confused or uninterested class despite your subject acumen and good intentions. If you are in business, all of your vision, skills, abilities, drive, determination, and courage will see you fall far short of success if you don't constantly hone your communication skills. It should be — by far — the skill set on which we work most diligently, for it has the highest payoff. Your ability to communicate, persuade, negotiate, build consensus, listen, speak confidently in a meeting, and build rapport with all types of people will also serve you greatly in times of turmoil and change. Ask yourself how effective you are at those core communication skills. An honest assessment of your skills is the clear starting place for positive personal change. When you use your skills effectively, you will become the person through which information is filtered in times of change. You become a person whom people can count on to help them clarify their own thoughts about the change, and you put yourself in position to be looked to for leadership.

Make Contact with all Levels of Your Organization

Communication also means building your informal network. Make sure you are building relationships with people throughout your organization. No matter what your position in the organization, don't be confined to your work team, your department, your management team, or your executive board. Building solid relationships up and down the company's organization chart and across departmental barriers can be invaluable when opportunities for leadership arise. You will create advocates throughout the organization who will be vital as you help lead an organization through the change process. Leaders who insulate themselves against the rest of their organization soon find themselves ineffective and neutralized. They don't walk around the organization enough, drop in on people in their offices, or invite people to visit theirs. They lose sight of how valuable it is to build those relationships in order to get unfiltered information, to hear what others in the organization are thinking and feeling, and to keep up to date on what's happening. This situation is actually a two-fold failure. Not only are leaders cutting themselves off from vital information, but the people they lead begin to see them as aloof and unapproachable. When change or crisis arises, getting commitment and buy-in from those employees could be exceedingly difficult.

It is important also to make strategic alliances across team and departmental lines no matter what your leadership position in an organization. If you are in sales, rest assured that making an ally in the accounting department has the potential to pay huge dividends someday in times of crisis or change. Effective change leaders are people who can create consensus across the organization. They are positioned and skilled to be natural diplomats in crisis. They are people who have the vision to see how plans affect all areas of an organization, and they have well-placed advocates throughout. Thus, when change is necessary, they are in a powerful position to lead it.

Work Smarter *and* Harder

One of the most misguided business clichés of the past decade is "work smarter, not harder." The truth is, really successful people do both. And I'm not talking about becoming a workaholic and getting your life all out of balance. Frankly, I think that people who can't get all of their work done in a 40-50 hour work week are not working hard enough while they are in the office! Working smarter and harder could be eating lunch in the cafeteria among other people so you can make those vital contacts rather than holing up alone in your office. It might mean listening to a tape series on time management and organization on the way home from work instead of the oldies station or talk radio. Really successful people have both the strategic thinking and fore-thought to work "smarter" while developing a stellar work ethic to take care of the "harder" part. The benefits related to change are actually threefold. First, you will simply accomplish more than most people, thus putting yourself in a positive position when the change monster rears its head. Second, you will be modeling positive behavior to others in the organization. Third, you will have already established patterns that will serve you well as your organization pushes through the sometimes painful and always exhausting change process. One company president I worked with said that the thing that surprised him most when his company went through a huge transition was the sheer amount of energy he expended in the process. It can truly be physically, mentally and emo-tionally draining to lead an organization through major change. Prepare yourself now for the physical and mental rigors you will face later. Work smarter AND harder, and start doing it right away.

Model a Steadfast Consistency of Character

Change — by its very nature — will bring about temporary chaos and instability. It can be very disconcerting to the average worker faced with this turmoil. As a leader, it will be necessary for you to be the anchor in that storm. People will look to you for stability and guidance. It is important that, during those tumultuous times, they know that they can trust what you say and do, that they can rely on your character in the midst of all the chaos. To thrive in the midst of change, you will need the cooperation of others. If they know they can count on you, they are more willing to give you that cooperation. It is never too late to start. Even if you find yourself in the midst of major change right now, start taking steps to model that consistency. Consistency of character means keeping commitments, dealing ethically with your subordinates and co-workers, and giving your best effort in whatever it is you are called on to do. It means having a steady temperament rather than moods that change with the direction of the wind. It means never asking your subordinates to do something you are unwilling to do yourself. Model the character you want to see in the people with whom you work, and you will be pleased to see it manifested in them over time. My favorite example of this is Winston Churchill. His character was constant before, during, and after the world-altering events of World War II, and he was an anchor for the British people as well as their allies. His character was thus modeled in the way his countrymen responded to the challenge. Likewise, when the change steps must be taken, you will be steady amidst the turmoil. This is an excellent place for a leader to be.

Thriving as a Leader in the Midst of Change

Having looked at vital steps in preparing for change, let's look at some key factors in thriving as a leader during change. If you have taken the strategic steps outlined in the previous section, you will be well prepared to take advantage of the opportunity change presents and to help your organization move positively and constructively through the change. While entire books have been written on this subject, there are three vital keys to effectively leading through change.

Be a Visionary

Organizations that effectively manage change are driven by a vision. It is the leaders in the organizations — both formal and informal leaders — who cast this vision, model this vision, and drive this vision. If you are in a position to help cast the vision, realize that three things must be in place before you can effectively move forward toward the vision — the "ABC's" of effective change:

- *Awareness* — individuals in the organization need to be aware that there is a problem with the status quo and that change is necessary. They have to understand that things simply cannot continue in the same way any longer. Without this awareness, there will never be any buy-in to the change vision.

- *Belief* — the organization must believe that the vision is the answer to the problem — that the plan the leaders have put into place is the best way to move to solution. Getting individuals to this belief level takes strong leadership and a great expenditure of energy. It is absolutely necessary, however, for change to take place effectively. Even a few individuals pulling against the vision can be disastrous for an organization.

- *Commitment* — individuals throughout the organization must buy into not only the vision as a whole, but they must also commit to their own role in seeing the vision through. Whether you are the vision-caster or a vision-advocate, your opportunities to shine as a leader are plentiful here.

Your job as a visionary entails ensuring that all three of these conditions are met. This takes a great deal of skill as a communicator. This is when the preparation you did leading up to the opportunity comes into play. The vision should be the filter through which all action in the company must pass. You must constantly bring that vision back into focus as different people get sidetracked into nonessential work, their own issues, and other peripheral concerns. Effective visionaries elicit a certain level of respect simply because they have a focus in the midst of the chaos of change. They become the natural anchors in a changing environment.

Be Solution Focused

It is vital in the midst of the turmoil you may be facing in a changing environment that you stay steadfast in your focus on solutions. Many times the circumstances surrounding significant corporate change are inherently negative, such as downsizing or a hostile takeover. In these instances it is very easy to get sucked into the negativity and to become focused on the problem. A leader simply cannot allow that to happen, no matter what the circumstances may be. No matter how negative a situation is, you can always find a positive response. Staying as solution-focused as possible will help you come up with positive responses. When I say this to a group of people in a seminar, I sometimes get disbelieving looks or even a comment suggesting that some situations are so negative that a positive response is not possible. My response to their skepticism is usually to refer them to the story of a remarkable leader of change named Candy Lightner. Some of you know her story. She is a woman who lost her 12-year-old daughter to a drunk driver in 1980. This was an almost unbearable tragedy. As a father, I frankly don't know how she even got out of bed the next day. Her response was to found Mother's Against Drunk Driving. In the next eight years, she went on to lead our entire society through a rather dramatic change. Her influence and leadership literally changed laws in our country and brought a horrible problem to the forefront of the American conscience. A true leader for change, she proves beyond a doubt that you can be positive and solution-focused, no matter how bad things are.

The other reason you must be solution-focused is that so few people are! Your organization needs as many people as possible keeping the vision in sight and focusing on solutions to the challenges it is facing. The bottom line is that most people are reactionary and problem-focused. You will stand out in contrast, and you will be a vital leader in a tumultuous time.

Communicate, Communicate, Communicate

Communication through change is vital on a variety of levels. The problem is that most people communicate less when faced with challenges. In the midst of change, particularly change with a negative cause, people often try to blend in to avoid being noticed. They try to ride out the storm while not rocking the boat. This bunker mentality flies in the face of the vital need for communication to occur at all levels. As you ensure that horizontal and vertical communication is happening effectively, you are adding credence to your position as an organizational leader. You are also helping to ensure that the process happens with as few hitches as possible. There are three main reasons communication is so vital during this process.

- *Leaders Need the Feedback.* It is vital that you seek constant feedback during organizational change. Not only do people need to feel the freedom to voice their concerns, but you also need an understanding of their perspective in order to lead them. Never assume that the way you see an issue is consistent with the way anyone else sees it. The truth is that perceptions vary widely, and we must keep constant lines of communication open so we can get vital feedback from those around us. This is the only way that we can move people toward solution and toward the vision that has been cast. Simply put, you cannot convince anyone of your solution if you don't know how other people view the problem. A huge failure among some leaders is to either assume everyone sees the problem their way, or to assume the difference in perspective doesn't matter.

- *People Need to Vent.* During organizational change, people are often bombarded with negative emotions — fear, anger, frustration, sadness. When kept bottled up, these emotions can be a time bomb ready to explode at the most inopportune moments. People need to know they can bring their concerns to the leadership of the organization without fear of retribution. They need to know that their feelings matter. This may be a little "soft" for some of you reading this, but it is the reality of the human condition. Leaders don't take it for granted.

- *Leaders Lead Through Communication.* This is not as elementary as it sounds. Your leadership is exhibited most readily by how you communicate with individuals and groups. Verbally, non-verbally, and vocally you need to be communicating positively and assertively throughout the change process. Ask questions. Give explanations when possible for why things are being done. Share the vision, and get the input of anyone who will give it to you.

The constantly changing nature of our society will never go away. Indeed the speed and frequency of change is increasing year by year. With this constant change come countless opportunities to shine as a leader. So check yourself, prepare yourself, and assert yourself; this changing world is in dire need of great leaders like you.

ABOUT
TIM BASS

*P*resident *of The Bass Consulting Group, a diversified speaking and training company with offices in Phoenix, Dallas and Atlanta, Tim Bass is considered by many to be simply one of the most substantive and entertaining speakers in America today. Through motivating keynotes, eye-opening seminars and personal consulting, he has helped thousands of people achieve measurably greater results. One client said, "You simply cannot experience one of Tim's sessions without coming away with something positive, significant and lasting." Calling on his experience in sales, management, and business ownership, Tim has worked closely with a host of diverse organizations. Tim currently serves as Director of Training for the Phoenix Suns and World Champion Arizona Diamondbacks. He holds degrees in Organizational Communication and English from Texas Tech University and his graduate work includes public speaking and education. He is a member of the American Society for Training and Development and is a constant student of success.*

Contact information:
Tim Bass
The Bass Consulting Group
2710 N. 60th Street
Scottsdale, AZ 85257
Phone: (602) 793-1596
E-mail: BassConsulting@earthlink.net

RESOURCE LISTING

Tim Bass
The Bass Consulting Group
2710 N. 60th Street
Scottsdale, AZ 85257
Phone: (602) 793-1596
E-mail: BassConsulting@earthlink.net

Louis B. Cady, M.D.
611 Harriet Street, Suite 304
Doctors Plaza
Evansville, IN 47710
Phone: (812) 429-0772
Fax: (812) 429-0793
E-mail: LCady@DrCady.com
Website: www.DrCady.com

Michael Connor
Creative Transitions
8 Nauset Road
Brockton, MA 02301
Phone: (508) 584-9062
Fax: (508) 580-6466
E-mail: MC@ThriveOnChange.com
Website: www.ThriveOnChange.com

Michelle Cubas
Positive Potentials, LLC
7120 E. 6th Avenue, #21
Scottsdale, AZ 85251
Phone: (480) 922-9699
Fax: (480) 663-6851
E-mail: MCubas@PositivePotentials.com
Website: www.PositivePotentials.com

Kathy Dempsey
The Learning Agenda
8317 Hamilton Oaks Drive
Chattanooga, TN 37421
Phone: (423) 894-8585
Fax: (423) 894-0071
E-mail: Kathy@TheLearningAgenda.com
Website: www.TheLearningAgenda.com

Nancy Hedrick, M.B.A.
ReGen Enterprises, LLC
12811 W. 131st Street
Overland Park, KS 66213
Phone: (913) 814-9504
Fax: (913) 685-7413
E-mail: Nancy@ReGen-Ent.com
Website: www.ReGen-Ent.com

Mark Hunter
MJH & Associates
15633 Underwood
Omaha, NE 68118
Phone: (402) 445-2110
Fax: (402) 445-0942
E-mail: MarkJHunter@email.msn.com

Jasun Light
BrainPower
P.O. Box 65478
Tucson, AZ 85728-5478
Phone: (520) 299-9999
E-mail: JasunLight@earthlink.net

Chet R. Marshall
Elevation Express
130 Summit Ridge
Hurricane, WV 25526
Phone: (304) 545-5100
Fax: (304) 757-5651
E-mail: Chetinwv@aol.com

Della Menechella
Personal Peak Performance Unlimited
8 Carmello Drive
Edison, NJ 08817
Phone: (732) 985-1919
Fax: (732) 572-2941
E-mail: Menech@DellaMenechella.com
Website: DellaMenechella.com

Carolyn Millet
Power of Politeness
P.O. Box 7058
Burlingame, CA 94011
Phone: (650) 340-9862
Fax: (650) 340-1287
E-mail: Carolyn@Polite.com
Website: www.Politeness.com

Barbara Mintzer
B.A. Mintzer & Associates
4019A Otono Drive
Santa Barbara, CA 93110
Phone: (800) 845-3211
Phone: (805) 964-7546
Fax: (805) 964-9636
E-mail: BMintzer@west.net
Website: www.BarbaraMintzer.com

Mike Monahan
M2HRA
1153 Bergen Parkway Suite M-181
Evergreen, CO 80439
Phone and Fax: (303) 674-3186
Voice Mail: (800) 759-2881
E-mail: M2HRA@aol.com

MaryAnn Morton
Morton Management, Inc.
327 Cahaba River Parc
Birmingham, AL 35243
Phone: (205) 972-8744
Fax: (205) 969-3595
E-mail: MaryAnn@adro.com

Cheryl Moser, Ph.D.
Cheryl Moser & Associates
P.O. Box 130963
Birmingham, AL 35213-0963
Phone: (205) 871-8644
Fax: (205) 879-8027
E-Mail: Cheryl@CherylMoser.com
Website: www.CherylMoser.com

Dondi Scumaci
Elevations Unlimited, Inc.
2438 Rim Oak
San Antonio, TX 78232
Phone: (210) 545-6277
E-mail:
 DScumaci@ElevationsUnlimited.com
Website: www.ElevationsUnlimited.com

Doug Smart, CSP
Doug Smart Seminars
P.O. Box 768024
Roswell, GA 30076
Phone: (770) 587-9784
Fax: (770) 587-1050
E-mail: Doug@DougSmart.com
Website: www.DougSmart.com

Liz Taylor, Ph.D.
Feel Good Seminars
2575 First Street
Lincoln, CA 95648
Phone: (916) 434-9460
E-mail: LizTaylorrd@yahoo.com
Website: www.Feel-Good-Seminars.com

Sam Waltz
Atlantic Leadership Institute
P.O. Drawer 3778
3920 Kennett Pike, Greenville Station
Wilmington, DE 19807-0778
Phone: (302) 777-4774
Fax: (302) 777-4775
E-mail: SamWaltz@SamWaltz.com
Website: www.AtlanticLeadership.com
         www.SamWaltz.com

Olita F. Williams
ATILO Training & Consulting Services
2647 Glenrose Hill
Atlanta, GA 30341-5785
Phone: (770) 938-4006
Fax: (770) 723-1498
E-mail: Atilofw@attglobal.net